Ethics
(and Other Liabilities)

Ethics
(and Other Liabilities)

Harry Stein

St. Martin's Press, New York

For my two Sadies, my mother and my daughter.
And for Priscilla

Library of Congress Cataloging in Publication Data
Stein, Harry.
  Ethics (and other liabilities)

    1. Ethics—Addresses, essays, lectures. I. Title.
BJ1012.S67   170   82-5580
ISBN: 0-312-26544-1   AACR2

The essays in this book first appeared in *Esquire* magazine.

Design by Andy Carpenter

Contents

Acknowledgments

A great many people contributed, in one way or another, to this book. I offer special thanks to Philip Moffitt and Lee Eisenberg, who enabled me to write "Ethics" in *Esquire* in the first place; to Byron Dobell and Priscilla Flood who edited me so capably there; to Ellen Fair, Will Tift and Lisa Bain for their patience and helpful suggestions; to Jay Acton, who has always been supportive; to Les Pockell of St. Martin's Press who believed in this project, and Susan Tennenbaum, who has helped bring it together. In the course of writing these essays, I have often called upon friends for advice and perspective. Among those to whom I am particularly indebted are Sybil Adelman, Martin Sage, David Black, Annie Reiner and Cary Schneider. And I thank those many individuals who, along the way, wrote me letters of encouragement. They made it all worthwhile.

On Becoming Mr. Ethics

In mid-1980, nine months into the life of the "Ethics" column I was writing on a monthly basis for *Esquire* magazine, I decided that it was time to pull back and examine the enterprise at hand. Now, nine months is not an extraordinarily long time as columns go—Drew Pearson's ran for thirty-seven years, and Art Buchwald will probably be turning out his on his deathbed—but given its unusual nature, and its unexpected impact on my own life, I felt such an exercise was called for.

An ethics column had, within the inner sanctums of *Esquire*, been a long time in gestation. I am told that the notion had first raised its hoary head several editors and two ownerships before, and had subsequently been passed on from regime to regime like some kind of ancient curse. I first learned of the idea shortly after the most recent management change in 1979. The incoming editor in chief appeared an earnest young man, but when the notion of an ethics column was pulled out of a broom closet and dusted off in his office, he reportedly snapped his fingers and lit up like a pinball machine. "Hey," he said, "I had damn near the same idea myself."

Five minutes later, the editor who had dragged the idea from the broom closet to the editor in chief suggested that I was the man for the job. This was a nice thing for the editor, who is my friend, to have done, but it was also unfathomable. Who was I to be handing down ethical judgments? I was, as my friend well knew, a congenital exaggerator and an occasional liar. I had never even taken an ethics course in college, opting instead to sign up for Sociology 52, Social Problems (T, Th, S at 8:00 A.M.), to fulfill my social sciences requirement.

When he proposed me for the job, my friend the editor did not mention any of this. "He's a basically thoughtful guy" is what he told the editor in chief, "and I promise you the column won't be boring. A subject like this, in the wrong hands, could be *really* boring."

"Thanks," I told him afterward, "but as it happens I have no idea how to make an ethics column interesting."

"Listen, just make it funny. Make a serious point every month, but stick in some laughs too."

Humor I could do. A humor column I had done. But still . . . funny ethics?

"Why not? We could even give you a pseudonym—Shecky Spinoza."

And that is pretty much how I approached it—not as a lark, exactly, but not as the weightiest proposition in the world either. The truth is, I'd have preferred to be given a humor column minus the serious point. But if this was the one they'd handed me, I was damn well going to make the best of it.

It did not take long to find out just how sticky a situation I had blithely strolled into.

As the subject for my initial column, I chose kissing

ass. This was a practice that I had always deemed loathsome, had railed against at a hundred dinner parties. But, now, obliged to set down 1,400 words putting the matter forever to rest, it suddenly looked to be all gray areas. In this society, don't people *have* to do it at least a little? Finally, whom does kissing up to people really hurt? Why *not* play the game?

So after completing a grim-faced, tough-as-nails first draft of the column, I sat down and rewrote it, equivocating. The final version had it both ways, taking the position that anyone who sucks up to superiors is a crud and that anyone who doesn't is something of a jackass.

Pretty nearly the same thing happened with the next effort and the one after that. The first draft would be dripping with righteous rage; then I'd get to thinking about it and soften it a little and, to be fair, a little more; then I'd go through it one more time to add the kidding around.

But, in fact, even as I strained over those early pieces, something else was going on.

During the height of Watergate, Jeb Magruder announced that the reason he found himself in such sorry circumstances was that somewhere along the line he had misplaced his "ethical compass." This inspired much mirth at the time—one columnist, I remember, called upon his readers to be on the lookout for Jeb's ethical compass—but there was something to what Magruder was saying, and it was applicable to a great many of us.

The fact is, very few people in this society make a habit of thinking in ethical terms; indeed, in many quarters, speaking about right and wrong is taken as prima facie evidence of softness—and "soft" is the one adjective that no American of stature or ambition needs to have associated with his name. That is the kind of thinking that has become general in this country, and Watergate was an almost inevitable consequence.

Nor were the values that motivated Nixon and his cronies so terribly different from the ones that drive millions of us in our professional and even our personal lives; looking out for number one invariably means that others get stepped on.

Yet, astonishingly, the notion that such behavior might be destructive is rarely raised, let alone seriously considered. Seemingly, we have reached the point where we are hardly aware of the possibility.

Well, suddenly, through no fault of my own but simply as a result of having to get out the appropriate number of words every month, there I was, obliged to look at the world with new—ethical—eyes. And it was a revelation. Questions that six months before would have seemed trivial or routine or utterly remote suddenly took on moral implications. Do I let the guy behind the cash register in the bookstore know that he has just mistakenly given the customer ahead of me a twenty-dollar bill instead of a five? Am I supportive of the friend who's cheating on his wife? Is there an appropriate individual response to a President who, with chilling cynicism, dangerously manipulates events to his political advantage? All at once there seemed a right and a wrong to everything—and an obligation to act on that knowledge.

Like some born-again humanist, I found myself bearing public witness to my new-found faith—occasionally to the mortification of my companions. Around Christmastime, I made a point of looking into the affiliations of all sidewalk Santas who crossed my path, discovering that those who claimed to be collecting for Cambodian relief were actually undercover Hare Krishnas. I took it upon myself to expose them single-handedly (though their faith permits them to solicit under what appear to be false pretenses, it forbids them to lie in response to direct questions about their beliefs). When calls to the news media and various governmental agencies initially proved fruitless, I took to standing beside them on street corners and subway platforms, sneering at them and warning people away.

A short while later, I launched a campaign against three-card monte hustlers, those sidewalk entrepreneurs, at the time pervasive in New York City, who invite passersby to relinquish their money in a rigged game. Though at first I imitated the tactics I'd successfully employed earlier, I became considerably more discreet when, one afternoon, one of the entrepreneurs retreated from the scene, visited a nearby construction site, and returned with a brick.

The entrepreneur did, of course, have a kind of point. Self-righteousness is a particularly loathsome trait—for years I myself had loathed individuals as disparate as Billy Graham and William Kunstler for flaunting theirs—and others could hardly be blamed for taking offense at mine. Indeed, that part of me that remained lucid found itself frequently twitching in embarrassment at some of the things it heard the rest of me saying.

But as Feodor D., that canny old fox, told us back in tenth grade, an obsession is an obsession, and eventually, unapologetically, this one found its way into the column. Looking again, I discovered that even the murkiest of grays resolved on closer examination into either black or white. Certainly there were times when adultery might appear a reasonable option—as in the case of the woman I spoke to who detested her husband, absolutely loathed the son of a bitch, but had two children and no marketable skills—but it is still a fundamentally rotten thing to do, it is still behavior that debases. Suddenly, abruptly, that was as obvious as an ad for Bon Jour jeans. It is simply that in a society in which moral and ethical laissez-faire (otherwise known as "Hey, if it works for you . . .") has been elevated to a national credo, it had become terribly easy to lose track of the obvious.

Inevitably, too, all of this had an impact on my personal life. When I was in the midst of grappling with the adultery question for the column, I sought the counsel of a woman I knew well and hoped to know better.

"Being unfaithful? I think it's unforgivable," she said, with impressive certainty. Then she paused. "Wait a minute, does this apply to you and me?"

"I don't know," I said. "Does it?"

"Well . . . I'm still seeing that other guy, you know."

"I haven't exactly been celibate myself."

But very quickly, we decided that it should apply to us. And it does. We are married now, with a child.

"You remind me," kidded a friend recently, "of Thomas More. Once he became Lord Chancellor of England, this guy, who was supposed to accede to the king's every wish, suddenly became an utter fanatic on behalf of the issues." He laughed. "Talk about taking a job seriously."

There is—I refer you to Sir Thomas's neck—such a thing as taking one's job *too* seriously, and that was a charge that others pressed on me with mounting frequency. Several people whom I'd known for years greeted my new attitude with derision or anger. "How dare you?" raged one, a fellow who'd been cited under an alias as a negative example in one essay. "The gall, the utter presumption, of your making these kinds of moral judgments!" Another friend, spotting a light piece I'd written in *Playboy*, called me long-distance expressing relief that I had not yet completely lost my sense of humor. One chum began referring to me, with more sarcasm than bonhomie, as Mr. Ethics.

These were observations to which I was acutely sensitive, but I came to realize too that in some ways, filling the column every month was simply a no-win proposition. Bertrand Russell himself might often have looked like a goody-two-shoes if he had tried to work out these issues neatly. Moreover, I sensed more than a little defensiveness in the excessively hostile reactions. It is not news that compromises come as easily to many as sleep after a trying day; it was now clear that a lot of those people do not like to be reminded of that fact. I was no longer surprised to run across friends who treaded gingerly on conversational terrain where once we frolicked.

But there were also considerable compensations. The mail in response to the column—and there was a great deal—revealed the vastness of the reservoir of hope and conscience that still exists in this land. There was the letter from the jocular fellow recounting in fascinating detail his bungled first—and last—experience as a shoplifter; and the one from the young mother wondering how to keep her child untainted by racism; and my favorite of all, the short note on elegant stationery from the woman in Ojai, California, whose husband, a once prominent literary agent, had been blacklisted and who never thought she'd live to see the day when ideals and idealism made the pages of a national magazine.

I never got such mail when I wrote my humor column.

But there was another kind of response to the column that was even more intriguing. "There are," as a woman I hardly know put it a few weeks ago, by way of self-definition, "a lot of closet ethical people. It's hard to speak up for something merely because it's right—you're always afraid of looking silly. Well, it's nice to have a bit of reinforcement."

This notion that one has to overcome peer pressure or simple embarrassment in order to act properly arose with surprising frequency. It is, of course, a melancholy thought: My God, are we really *that* far gone?

But then I stop and consider my own case. It was, after all, only a matter of months since I'd gotten over the embarrassment myself.

Kiss, Kiss, Grovel, Grovel

The summer of 1976 was gaudy with spectacle, what with the Bicentennial and Entebbe, but as far as I was concerned, the most entertaining divertissement of all was the sight of a string of Democratic vice-presidential aspirants trekking down to Plains, Georgia, to be looked over by Jimmy Carter, about to be nominated for President. After each meeting, Carter led his guest from the house into the front yard to meet the assembled press, and each senator, wearing uncharacteristically casual clothes (just like the ones Jimmy wore) and glancing Jimmy's way as he spoke, blithely proceeded to lose his dignity. John Glenn kept repeating how happy he was to be there; old Ed Muskie, facing what would surely be his last shot at national office, said that he and Jimmy were on the same "wavelength"; Walter Mondale—his chances apparently in jeopardy because some Carter advisers regarded him as too liberal—explained that he had never really supported busing after all but only believed in upholding the rulings of the courts.

Now, as groveling goes, this was pretty tame stuff. In Iran, members of the Majlis—the old Iranian parliament that was dissolved when the current bunch took over—used to stand up and cheer every time the shah ordered them to enact a new piece of legislation, and later, when they were told by the Ayatollah that all they had to do to be granted amnesty was to write out a complete list of their crimes, they stood up and cheered again.

Still, there was something disheartening about the Plains thing, about witnessing a group of men—whose fondest dream it was to lead the forces of freedom—plastering their faces with little grins and toadying to someone they hardly knew.

But what was even more disheartening was the public response to this spectacle: No one seemed to mind it a bit. Indeed, most of what little press comment there was at the time praised Carter, for experimenting with the awkward selection process, and his guests, for making themselves so readily available as guinea pigs.

Those of a cynical cast of mind would, of course, maintain that anyone who expected some other reaction had to be a fool.

"You," my friend Ralph told me back then, when I expressed some disappointment over the events in Plains, "are a fool." Ralph paused for a moment and considered. "You are also a pompous prig. Kissing ass happens to be the lifeblood of the system, the vehicle in which one rides up every corporate ladder. Sycophancy is what keeps America moving."

An overstatement, perhaps. Still, I have thought about it a good deal since and it is, finally, hard to argue with Ralph's jaundiced overview.

The syndrome becomes apparent as early as the third grade: There's always that one damnable kid, that one wimp, whose arm is constantly in the air, straining so desperately to please that it looks as if it might pop out of its socket. In college, the number of sycophants inexplicably multiples by five or six or seven times, with only a modest change in their modus operandi: Instead of answering questions, they *ask* them—in an eager, bright-eyed way that is supposed to convey interest. By the time one begins working, it seems that almost everyone is looking for an edge—smiling too much or trying too hard to be seen working late or agreeing too readily with idiot superiors or waiting for superiors to pronounce an opinion before offering up one's own.

But at what cost? Is it possible to spend a good part of every day tailoring one's behavior to fit the tastes of others and at the same time remain—deep down where the bosses' eyes don't shine—independent, self-determined, pure?

That is not an easy question to answer, and it's no wonder that, when confronted with it, many people prefer to deal with the far simpler question of motivation. "My boss not only wants flattery, he needs it," a woman bank teller of my acquaintance says, "so when I flatter him, I basically regard it as his problem."

"Listen," agrees a friend of hers, an advertising copywriter, "the higher up people are, the more insecure they tend to be. The simple fact is, people almost always vie for promotions as much on the basis of politics as merit."

"There's a fine line," adds someone else, "between servility and diplomacy. When you don't know how to relate to a superior, being obsequious is the easiest way."

"Do you *have* to kiss ass to get ahead?" asks Ralph today. "Well, in most places there's maybe one guy who doesn't. Either he's very, very good or he's the boss's son."

Okay, fine. In the wide world of self-justification, all

such excuses wear very well. This *is* an imperfect planet. Sometimes you *do* have to give a little. Who can argue with aphorisms?

But, oddly, the point, the elusive point, comes more sharply into focus with every such conversation; each act of evasion is itself evidence of the subtly degenerative process. In the end, the fact is immutable: With every unfunny joke laughed at, with every liaison established primarily for ambition's sake, one gives away a bit of soul.

Let us turn, for just a moment, to the specter of Ed McMahon, certainly among the most successful yes-men in history. Ed's job, as every schoolchild knows, is to guffaw loudly and applaud a lot and do whatever else has to be done to keep someone else's ego soaring. Over the years, Ed has done this so often and so well that, as one watches him on TV, he appears to fawn by second nature. A writer named Harry Shearer, who observed Ed at work with Jerry Lewis during the muscular dystrophy telethon, offers vivid confirmation of that impression in *Film Comment:*

> Whether he's with Johnny or Jerry, he assumes the air of someone who's totally absorbed in the proceedings. . . . When Chad Everett introduces the president of Olympia Beer to Jerry, Ed knows he's not on camera. But he still does a big "Do-you-hear-who-this-is?-Can-you-believe-this-man-is-actually-here?-Well-let's-hear-it-for-him!" take to the audience and starts clapping loudly. It's not his job. . . . It's just the little something extra you get when you use Ed.

That, of course, is the big danger in kissing ass too assiduously: the possibility of being *seen* as a servile wretch.

Hubert Humphrey's problem, the thing that perhaps cost him the presidency, was not so much that he had slipped a vital piece of his anatomy into Lyndon Johnson's pocket—*that* he had done gladly—but that the act had been so utterly public. In offices around the country, young executives on the make have much the same difficulty: Too obviously eager to impress the higher-ups, they alienate legions of contemporaries, who take to standing around the water cooler muttering darkly.

The truly accomplished sycophants, the ones who quickly move on to become kissees themselves, curry favor so deftly that it passes for simple courtesy or tact or insight or charm. "When I meet someone who's going to be my employer," says a talented reporter at a Chicago newspaper, a young man who plays the game as well as anyone I've ever known, "I ask myself, 'How can this person be had?' With my last editor, I immediately sensed that he was looking to be fatherly, so I made myself into the journalist son he always wanted. It instantly became in his interest to maximize my options at the paper—and I don't think any of my peers even noticed."

But the psychic dues such sycophants pay are as great as those levied upon obsequious assistant clerks or fawning retainers to the wealthy or even the cringing clones who pass for sales help at certain snotty Fifth Avenue shops—sometimes greater because they are usually so much more self-aware. The reporter in question has invested almost $20,000 in therapy, and only now is he beginning to come up with a rationalization for his behavior that he can swallow. "The bottom line," he says, "is self-respect. I understand what I'm doing, and that makes it okay. There are only a few things worth putting yourself on the line for in any given year, anyway." He pauses. "Frankly, I think people who don't kiss ass at least a little in this society are masochistic."

That is a noxious little thought—one that sets the gut to churning—but it is, of course, a sentiment that is being expressed with increasing frequency these days, most notably in those dismal tracts with the cunningly designed covers that urge their readers to take power at the expense of others and always to look out for number one. Unhappily, it's even beginning to get to a lot of people who should know better.

I recently visited a friend I'll call Rudolph Corvin, hitherto one of the most contented people in this world, in the midtown New York office of the large life insurance company in which he has worked at a middle-level job for nine years. After a while, I asked him about this business of ass kissing.

"Oh, no," said Rudolph, "I would never do that. I just do my work as well as I can, wait for my boss to notice, and hope that someone above me will come down with a debilitating disease." He paused and looked forlornly around his little cubicle. "That's how I got where I am today, by waiting for people to get sick."

Uncommon Decency

It was one of those days that mercifully seem to come to New York just once each spring, a day of rain so heavy that it obscured vision and rushed over gutters onto sidewalks already strewn with umbrellas destroyed by the wind.

I was late, and more than a little annoyed; there was no shelter at the Seventy-sixth Street and Lexington Avenue bus stop, where I waited, and my umbrella, too, was threatening to collapse.

Finally the bus arrived. I handed the driver my transfer, wiped the water from my glasses, and began to move toward the rear.

"Hey, buddy," came the shout.

I continued walking.

"Hey, *you*, get back here!"

I noticed a few pairs of eyes staring my way. "Are you talking to me?" I asked.

"Who does it look like I'm talking to?" The driver motioned me back. "That'll be seventy-five cents. This transfer is valid only if you catch the bus at Seventy-ninth Street." Technically he was, of course, correct; such a regulation certainly exists in a book somewhere.

"But I get on here all the time," I protested.

"I don't give a damn what you do. Seventy-five cents or get off the bus."

So I gave him his money—and a good deal more than that in abuse. "You know," I said, taking a seat behind him, "it's people like you who give this city such a lousy reputation. What's the difference if I get on here—especially on a day like this?"

There was no response. Indeed, with the wall of plastic between us, I was not even sure he'd heard. "You son of a bitch," I muttered.

He had heard. A moment later a huge hand was on my shoulder. "One more word from you and I'm throwing you off. I don't have to take that from no one."

For the rest of the ride I reserved my comments for the elderly gentleman beside me. I said that I hoped I had ruined the driver's day.

He smiled benignly. "That's not a very nice sentiment," he said.

"Why shouldn't I feel that way? He's ruined mine."

And, indeed, it was hours before that sense of irritation and dismay left me, days before I was able to talk about the encounter without wishing I were massive enough to have *dared* the guy to throw me off his bus. And it was weeks before it occurred to me that maybe I'd acted almost as badly as he had.

Mine was not a particularly strict upbringing—my parents did a lot of cajoling—but in our house certain rules of behavior were never in question. It was assumed that one was always solicitous of people's feelings and ready to offer comfort, and contemptuous of those who cavalierly slighted others. "Always," went my mother's admonition (which to a four-year-old did not sound like a cliché), "put yourself in the other person's shoes."

In retrospect, I see that this was, as much as anything else, a matter of politics. My parents, children of immigrants, raised in relative poverty, were of the fervent conviction that the world was divided between people who cared about others and people who did not, between the generous-spirited and the petty, between us and them. Thus it was that in their teens they became radicals, marching on behalf of the Scottsboro Boys; that in their twenties they campaigned for FDR; that in their thirties, after the coming of Jackie Robinson, they became fervent Brooklyn Dodgers fans. Thus it was, too, that in her sixties my mother spotted from her bedroom window a local newspaper vendor being hustled away by the police for having an improper license. Though extremely ill, she dashed out of bed to help him, then spent the next two days phoning city agencies on his behalf.

I now realize that it is naive to estimate the contents of people's hearts on the basis of their political affiliations—though seeing any gathering of Reagan Zealots always gives me renewed pause—but the principle remains valid: if one is to lay any claim to character, he must live his convictions daily, reflexively, in a hundred tiny ways. "I stopped seeing a man because he was rude to waiters," reported a woman of my acquaintance, and I understood perfectly. Someone without respect for waiters or salesclerks or business subordinates is unquestionably going to be found wanting on all the big issues. Indeed, when Jimmy Carter was in office, one woman I know actually turned against him because she had heard somewhere that Rosalynn had a habit of hiding stale crackers in corners to gauge the efficacy of maids. "I worked as a maid in a hotel one summer," she said. "I know all about the indecency of people like that."

On the face of it, showing consistent consideration for others should not seem a terribly difficult proposition. It truly doesn't require much more energy to be thoughtful than to be thoughtless, to be a small presence for good instead of just another schlump on the street.

But somehow it seems that fewer and fewer of us are able to manage it. Indeed, we seem to behave worse toward one another today than we ever have before. There was a time, well within memory, when certain elementary rules of human intercourse were enforced in this society by popular assent, when not to abide by them was to be regarded as a lout or worse: Just a generation or so ago, virtually no citizen over the age of sixty would ever have been obliged to stand on a crowded bus or subway. Today the public conveyances are full of elderly standees while kids and teenagers and legions of young men and women in designer jeans sit staring blankly ahead. We have, quite simply, become a society where lack of consideration is the norm, where it is entirely legitimate to give a damn only about oneself.

What is particularly curious about all of this is that there is a good deal more warmth in the air now than ever before. Every time we dial Information, some operator tells us to have a good day; "Have a Coke and a smile," recommends one electronic voice; "Reach out, reach out and touch someone," advises another. It is almost as if the reduction to ad copy of expressions of human need has rendered us less capable of actually responding to others. Incessantly bombarded by platitudes, we simply don't listen so well anymore or see so clearly or, finally, feel so deeply.

It is, to be sure, a grim picture, and there is little reason to believe it will soon change. So we are left with our consciences, each of us having to choose whether we will, in fact, reach out and touch someone or simply continue to look the other way.

Those who choose right can do an inestimable amount of good—can, indeed, set even cynical strangers to speculating on the possibilities of the human heart.

At dusk on the Friday of Labor Day weekend, 1973, ten miles short of Indianapolis, the old Chevy in which my girlfriend and I had driven from the East Coast to the West and nearly back again finally gave out. Almost out of money, we limped into a gas station off the highway. The owner-mechanic's diagnosis came in five minutes: our drive shaft was shot; we needed a new one.

My face fell. "How much will that cost?" I asked.

He studied us—disheveled twenty-four-year-olds with a pair of anti-Nixon bumper stickers on our useless vehicle—for a moment. "Wait here," he said. And then, to his assistant, "Eddie, I'll be back in a while."

Although according to Eddie the place was due to close for the weekend in an hour, the owner was gone for three hours, until after 10:00 P.M., and when he returned it was with a drive shaft for our Chevy. A *used* drive shaft, found, we eventually understood, after a search of every junkyard and auto graveyard in town.

"How much do we owe you?" I asked finally. Then,

quickly, I added, "We only have thirty-five dollars; we'll send you the rest."

He furrowed his brow. "Well, let's see," he said. "It'll cost you another fifteen bucks for gas to get to New York, and you'll need a motel room tonight, and you've gotta eat. . . . Let's say seven dollars."

"Seven dollars? That's ridiculous."

"Nope, seven dollars it is."

After I'd stopped resisting and paid him his money, he clapped a hand on my shoulder and smiled a smile I'll remember years after the bitterness of the run-in with the bus driver has left me. "Have a good weekend," he said.

A
Life
in Crime

One long-ago August afternoon at Camp Indian Hill—
it must have been during rest period—the talk in my bunk
turned to crime.

We were for it.

"I once stole sixteen albums from a record store in one
afternoon," reported Richie Hart. "Sixteen!"

Petey Stillman was dubious. "Where was this?" he
asked.

"In Buffalo. I was with my mother and stepfather on
their honeymoon." Richie chuckled. "Sixteen! The guy
never knew what hit him."

"That's nothing," retorted Neil Pollock from his bunk
across the room. "Me and a couple of friends once swiped a
portable TV set."

"No shit?"

"It was easy. We just walked into Sears and walked
out with it, just as if it belonged to us. No one said a thing."

"Wow," said Allen Bloomgarten, "that's amazing.
The most I ever steal is candy. I'm chicken."

"Me too," admitted Johnny Paulz, the guy below me,

with regret. Craning his neck, he looked up at me. "How about you, Stein?"

I hesitated. "I've never stolen anything."

"Come off of it."

"No, really, I haven't."

"Bullshit," snapped Allen. "What do you think, we're gonna turn you in?"

They all laughed.

"Can't you guys even imagine someone not stealing?" I asked.

Allen paused for a moment and thought that over. "No."

That scene occurred more than twenty years ago—two months before Willie McCovey lined out to Bobby Richardson to end the 1962 World Series, when John Kennedy was President, when a lot of us believed the world was moving along quite splendidly—and I look upon it with the special fondness Warren Beatty must feel for his first timid childhood crush.

It is a cliché of the early 1980s—one repeated as casually as the observation that James Watt is scary or that eggs are bad for you—that the nation has been on a steady decline from that time to this. The problem is not that people are no longer able to distinguish between right and wrong; it is simply that they have decided it is much easier to avoid doing so. Jimmy Carter, who apparently gave these things more thought than the rest of us, speculated that our "moral decline"—his phrase—began the day Kennedy was shot, and he was probably right. Things have never been quite the same since.

But there are 200 million stories in the naked society,

and what is called the national state of mind is the sum total of all of them. I know precisely when my personal moral decline began, for the awful incident that triggered it is as vivid in my mind as those unforgettable photos of the bloated bodies in Jonestown. It was a freezing Saturday morning in the winter of 1964, Lyndon Johnson's third or fourth month in office. Walking out of a large stationery and toy store called Big Top, near my home in New Rochelle, New York, I pulled my gloves from my coat pocket, and a candy wrapper, stuffed there days before, fluttered to the ground. In an instant, an employee of the store was upon me, dragging me back inside by the scruff of the neck as if I were some urchin out of Dickens. "I got you," he screamed, "I finally got one of you." My neck was pulsating, and a gaggle of onlookers had gathered before someone finally held aloft the empty candy wrapper and I was grudgingly released.

In order to understand the dimensions of this humiliation, it is necessary to know just how self-satisfied an adolescent I had by this time become. What I had told my bunkmates back at Indian Hill was true. I never *had* stolen, not even once. My thinking on the subject had been shaped early, by my mother, who was a warm, blunt, humorous ex-Communist with an unyielding view of the proper order of things. Stealing, as far as she was concerned, was for degenerates—something a politician's kids might do, not hers. Thus it was that when, as a six-year-old, I had happened upon a child's plastic wallet containing two dollars in a field near our home, I was made to leave it there for two weeks on the extraordinarily unlikely chance that its owner would be back looking for it. A few years later, after I'd almost killed myself screeching my bike to a halt in heavy traffic to retrieve a twenty-dollar bill lying in the gutter, I was obliged to take it to the police station. By my fifteenth year, having been raised on such stuff, I wore an air of moral rectitude as casually as I wore my corduroy pants with the too-short legs.

But the incident at the Big Top store changed all that; though the bruises the bastard left on my neck were gone in a week, I was marked in other, subtler ways. Ten days later, I returned to the store and, gushing perspiration, made off with an Official Clincher Double Header softball.

After that it got easier, then easier still, and pretty soon the guilt was just about gone. Indeed, by the late Sixties, theft was regarded in many quarters as a birthright. Property, according to the logic of the era, was evil, so taking property had to be a dandy thing to do. No one I knew was ever able to explain with precision the connection between My Lai and Woolworth's, the favorite local target, but, then, very few explanations were being called for; in those days, as in these, cynicism bred cynicism. For those with an ineradicable residue of remorse, there was the comfort of an additional rationale, a more pragmatic one: Storekeepers didn't really lose out because shoplifting was always accounted for as overhead.

I was never a big-time operator myself, never ripped off clothing, or, as in the case of one acquaintance—an SDS heavy at my school—entire stereo systems, on order. Cat-like, I would prowl the occasional supermarket, grabbing a roll of Scotch tape here, a can of sardines there, slipping them into my pants, and stealing away. Then, too, I would charge the odd long-distance call to one of the credit card numbers revealed in the local underground paper—IBM's or, for some reason, Paul Newman's—but I supposed the telephone scam to be not quite the same thing.

I was never caught, never even suspected, until a year after I'd finished school. I was passing a few months in Paris, freelancing, and early on, I'd taken to dropping by Le Drugstore on the Boulevard des Italiens in search of newly arrived American magazines; they were, I reasoned—for I still preferred to have a rationale—exorbitantly priced, and anyway, with their lack of vigilance, the capitalist proprietors offered a virtual invitation to steal.

So there I was one afternoon, a copy of the latest *Sports Illustrated* rolled in my sweaty hand, strolling out the door toward the Place de l'Opéra, when I was accosted by the store manager. He was irate, in French. *"Voleur! Je vous ai vu!"* he cried, and I allowed myself to be led to the local *commissariat de police*.

There I was deposited before the desk of a detective who was casually dressed and lightly bearded, no more than a couple of years older than I. I relaxed. The manager, raving, gave his version of the story and stormed out. The detective turned to me. I smiled and shrugged. *"Je suis désolé,"* I apologized, "but it's so hard to find any reliable information in Paris about American sports."

His eyes darkened. *"Taisez-vous!"* he cut me off. "Shut up! What do you think, this is a joke?" And a moment later, I found myself in a little cell with all the other shoplifters nabbed in the district during the previous hour: There were a pair of French teenagers working as a team, a Spaniard, and one man of early middle age in a Cardin suit, sitting on the bench, sobbing. He had, he explained, been caught trying to steal a skirt for his wife from Au

Printemps, the department store, during his lunch hour, and now, an hour overdue at the office, he was sure he would lose his job.

I sat in that cell for a good hour and a half, feeling giddy, then chagrined, then apprehensive, and, finally, more than a little slimy. By the time I was released, with a simple admonition ("Do it again and, *pffft*, you'll be on the next plane to New York"), my relief mingled with self-loathing. Though for the next month I got itchy every time I passed Le Drugstore—old habits die hard—my criminal career in Paris was over.

Nor did it resume on my return to the States, for, in fact, honesty turned out to be a habit, too, and a much more congenial one. Not only did I eschew shoplifting, but I didn't even take up the adult variation favored by so many veterans of the Sixties, grown successful and cautious: the phony expense account. Financially, this may have been imprudent, but it at least enabled me to blast Richard Nixon, who was just then wading into Watergate, with an uncluttered conscience.

Indeed, within months I had become, in a subdued, unostentatious way, every bit as self-righteous as I'd been that day I'd walked into Big Top a decade before. And I suppose I remain that way.

Just the other week, a new acquaintance, aware of my professional interest in the subject, was reminiscing about his shoplifting past. "I was no slouch," he was saying. "In supermarkets, I'd always go right for the most expensive meats. During my salad days, I ate only steak." He laughed. "The only trouble was, when I hid the packages in my clothes, the juice always seemed to seep out. My whole wardrobe was marked by stains of guilt."

"And do you," I asked with the feigned casualness of the born again, "still do it?"

He must have caught something in my eye. "Uhh, yeah, once in a while. Just little things." He smiled wanly. There was a long silence. "I guess I'm really a schmuck, aren't I?"

The
Big A

A bunch of us guys were sitting around one night, like refugees from a Löwenbräu commercial, talking about—what else?—women. We liked 'em, liked 'em a whole lot. Couldn't get enough of 'em, in fact. But then one of the guys got a kind of twisted look on his face, and he said that a few weeks earlier he'd had a chance to start something with someone very special, but he hadn't done it. So we all asked why. And he shrugged his shoulders and looked a little sheepish. "She was living with some guy. I just couldn't get used to the idea of her going home to him still smelling of me."

Honest to God, that's an actual verbatim quote. And maybe we weren't so much like the guys in the Löwenbräu ads after all, because, dumb as it sounded, no one laughed when he said it. I think we all more or less understood how the guy felt. Romantic comedies notwithstanding, these situations almost always end up more melodrama than bedroom farce, with someone's ego lying on the carpet; only genuine Löwenbräu guys saunter cavalierly into messes like that.

Just recently, at dinner at the home of a friend, I found

myself sitting across from a strikingly intelligent woman who had dark hair, luminous green eyes, and the most unmistakably flirtatious manner this side of Scarlett O'Hara.

"Where do you live?" I asked at the end of the evening. "I'll call you."

She smiled. "That'd be nice. I should tell you, though, I'm married." A beat. "But it doesn't bother me, if it doesn't bother you."

"Uhhh. . . ."

The cliché, as I'd been raised on it, had never worked like *that*. Think back on any episode of "Love, American Style"; the scenario almost never changed: The man was the bounder, his wife or girlfriend the victim, and the other woman some manner of shrew, though once in a while, when played with great angst, she might pass for victim number two.

And for years the cliché was a not inaccurate reflection of real life. During one period of her life, a friend I'll call Barbara, now in her late thirties, was involved with so many married men that she took to referring to herself as "the adultery specialist."

"Every single adulterous relationship," she insists now, "was exactly the same. Even the dialogue never changed: 'I wish I'd met you (fill in the blank) years ago,' and, of course, 'I never knew it could be like this.' The wife would always commit suicide if he left her and she always hated sex, but she was someone I'd like a lot if I ever met her."

Now, often as not, it is the husband or boyfriend who gets screwed, figuratively, as the literal antics proceed apace. This societal adjustment has not been an easy thing for some men to accept. "Jesus Christ," a fellow of my acquaintance recently complained upon learning that his wife had turned the tables on him, "where is Hester Prynne now that we need her?"

But the sad and quite obvious truth is that smarmy is smarmy, no matter who's at which end of the stick, and a great many women are finding out what great numbers of men have always known: It ain't much fun being the scoundrel. A book editor I know, a married woman fresh from one of those affairs featuring hotel one-nighters and restaurants where everyone manages to face the wall, emerged from the experience sounding like Fred MacMurray in *The Apartment.*

"The sneaking-around part wasn't too bad," she says. "What I couldn't stand was the guilt about my family. Do you know that I actually missed my son's birthday? And meanwhile I was leading this poor guy on, letting him believe that I might leave my husband."

And yet it continues, this avalanche of infidelity, this tidal wave of two-timing, outstripping the birth rate and the death rate, outstripping any rate you can think of, with the possible exception of Texaco's third-quarter earnings. Driven by despair or desperation or loneliness or horniness, we just cannot stop.

There are, of course, a lot of people who maintain that infidelity can be therapeutic; they use such terms as "safety valve," and "realism," and "irrepressible physical needs."

"It's damn easy to be self-righteous about it," as one guy I know puts it, "when you're not trapped in a deadend marriage." And, let's face it, some of what these people say seems to make a lot of sense. The French have gone so far as to devise an entire system of social relationships based on satisfying irrepressible physical needs without anyone ever having to be late for dinner.

But it is, I think, no coincidence that the French are as emotionally blocked as any people on the planet; that even in their most intimate relationships—spouse to spouse, parent to child—certain basic feelings and needs are rarely expressed. In France this is known as reserve; elsewhere it is called being screwed up. The bottom line, quite simply, is that it is impossible for people to compartmentalize their lives, to keep a single aspect of their existence under lock and key yet be blissfully open about the rest. Human beings don't function that way.

And yet, it seems so routinely to work out badly even when everyone plays it completely straight. "Sometimes," Katharine Hepburn was recently quoted as saying, "I wonder if men and women really suit each other. Perhaps they should live next door and just visit now and then." And she had Spencer Tracy!

We try variation after variation: marriage contracts, separate vacations, living together for years on end without marriage, and still, so often, there is the slow unraveling. "Let's see other people," one partner finally suggests—code for the fact that someone wants out—and the relationship limps along its melancholy way.

How, I wonder, did it work out so nicely for my grandparents? Hardly past childhood when they met, thoroughly unworldly, desperately poor, fixed up by a *matchmaker*, for God's sake, and they made it through sixty-odd years together, Papa and Mama. When my grandmother died, my grandfather, eighty-six and barely able to walk, still a socialist and exclusively a Yiddish speaker, came to live with us for a while. I am still haunted by the wail that came in the very early hours of the morning through the thin wall that separated our bedrooms: "Mama, Mama . . ."

It is, of course, those kinds of precedents that shine through the generations in almost every family, that keep us all believing in the happily ever after.

"Why," asked the most promiscuous woman I know, when I had told her about my grandparents, "can't people settle down with someone that way and be happy? That's all I want."

Why indeed. Well, for one thing, my grandfather didn't sit around in his yarmulke and prayer shawl lusting after Bo Derek. And, strongwilled as she was, the only career goal my grandmother ever had was to become the mother of a rabbi. A world without expectations, a world with clearly labeled slots, is hard to get lost in. They had each other, those two, and they knew how to be satisfied.

What is less obvious is that my grandparents might still have opted to be just as discontented as the rest of us. Indeed, my other grandfather, just a bit more American-ized, a bit more fluent in English, *was* something of a phi-landerer. I have in my possession a letter written in the mid-Forties from my father to my mother describing an attempt to reconcile her parents after one of their periodic splits:

> Ma told me she'd consider going back to him for a down payment of $500 to refurnish the apart-ment (which personally I consider steep even at wartime price levels) plus a guarantee of no more running around. Of course, she changed her mind in the next breath. Anyway, ten minutes after this conversation, Pop phoned with an offer of $1,000 plus a month's vacation, just the two of

them (with Yiddish vaudeville entertainment), and she's so bewildered she says all right. So after a bit of hemming on the phone, he says he'll come right over, and does. So for a while things are all right. I keep the ball rolling, talking about this and that and events of the day; then I go to bed. They remained on more or less businesslike terms, and I could hear a lot of whispering about let's get down to business and how's about furnishing the apartment, and she gets a down payment of $50, I think, and he sleeps over only two rooms away, which for them is like having an orgy. . . .

I discovered that note two weeks after emerging from a long relationship—one that had been marked by a little adultery and a lot of acrimony—and if the note wasn't quite comforting, at least it put things in perspective. Even in relatively simpler times, one's world was obviously of one's own making.

When it comes to infidelity, we have seven millennia of human history to draw upon, and the evidence appears conclusive: Duplicity, no matter how it's dressed up, generally makes most everyone involved feel rotten. The alternative—nurturing trust and trying not to let it wither—is, God knows, nothing like a sure thing either, and it's a hell of a lot more work, but what choice do we have?

Racial Slurs, Ethnic Jokes

The New York journalism scene was considerably enlivened early this past summer when abruptly, in the midst of a protracted heat wave, staffers on *The Village Voice* began tearing one another up in print. This diverting spectacle, which ultimately led to public accusations of censorship, homophobia, and general meanness of character, was touched off by a Jules Feiffer cartoon in the June 25 issue of the paper.

Like so much of the estimable Feiffer's work, the offending cartoon depicted a character—in this case a bull-necked blue-collar type—caught up in an interior monologue. "Can't say 'fag' anymore," he complains in the first illustration. "Can't say 'dyke' anymore," he adds in the second. By the end of the strip, he is utterly fed up: "I can only take so much tolerance." A pause. "I'm going back to 'nigger.'"

"Whatever its intentions," said an open letter signed by fourteen *Voice* staffers and contributors in the very same issue, "the cartoon plays into, and not off, a reactionary sensibility. We find it not only offensive but far from funny and not in the least illuminating."

And we were off to a battle that would rage with increasing fury for another month, until all the combatants evidently left for vacation.

Watching from the sidelines, it was difficult not to be struck by the self-indulgence of it all—and by the extraordinary self-righteousness of so many of the participants. Any casual follower of the quirky goings-on would have had every right to conclude that the *Voice* harbors more sober-sided prigs than the National Women's Christian Temperance Union.

In this particular case, the moralizing also served to divert attention from the merits of what Feiffer had been saying, which is a pity. The issue of racism resurgent is a very real one. But, in fact, a strong case can be made that the cartoon was inaccurate in two essential ways: first, in suggesting that bigotry is fundamentally the province of blue-collar types, and second, and more to the point, by indicating that some of us are shy about expressing ourselves on the subject. In my experience, that has not been true for quite a while now.

To be sure, in what passes as enlightened circles, it is all done quite deftly. No one goes around at cocktail parties referring to blacks as "niggers," and virtually no one bears them exactly that kind of contempt. But there are the quiet asides, and the jokes, that subtly divide the world into "them" and "us."

Just the other day, a man I'll call Jeffrey Stillman, someone I have known since elementary school, a veteran of half a dozen civil rights marches, grinned at me over dinner. "I got a quiz for you: A heavy black guy and a light black guy jumped from the top of the Empire State Building at the exact same instant. Who hit the pavement first?"

"Who?"

"Who cares?"

Now, this fellow will swear on his grandmother's head that he is not racist and mean it. He would *still* march in civil rights marches if there were any left. He still gets misty-eyed when he hears "We Shall Overcome." So do I.

"I'm afraid," I told Jeffrey some minutes later, "that Mrs. Levin would be ashamed of us."

Mrs. Levin was our fourth-grade teacher at Roosevelt Elementary School in New Rochelle, New York. Though Roosevelt was, in those prebusing days, a virtually all-white school—the only black faces on the premises belonging to the children of the Ghanaian ambassador to the U.N.—Mrs. Levin was passionate on the subject of race relations. Where other fourth-grade classes would take a break for show and tell, we would listen to Sammy Davis Jr. sing, "You've got to be taught to hate and fear," on the Victrola; where other classes would hear the poems of Joyce Kilmer or Sara Teasdale, we would get Langston Hughes or Countee Cullen. Her favorite was a Cullen poem entitled "Incident":

> Once riding in old Baltimore,
>   Heart-filled, head-filled with glee,
> I saw a Baltimorean
>   Keep looking straight at me.
>
> Now I was eight and very small,
>   And he was no whit bigger,
> And so I smiled, but he poked out
>   His tongue, and called me, "Nigger."

I saw the whole of Baltimore
From May until December;
Of all the things that happened there
That's all that I remember.

Up until the afternoon that Mrs. Levin read it to us, I am not sure I had ever heard the term "nigger," but I instantly understood that there was something obscene about it, that it was viler than any curse word, more debasing than any oath.

And for years, throughout the Fifties and the Sixties, no one I knew would ever have used the word or said anything else that might be interpreted as racist. Oh, sure, most of us had few black friends, or none, might even have felt ill at ease in predominantly black gatherings, but the impulse was always toward bridging the gap, not fishing around in it for easy laughs.

Suddenly I was conscious of how very much we had lost. "What is it," I asked Jeff, "that made us change?"

He shrugged. "Oh, just history." And he talked about the shift in the attitude of white liberals in general as the civil rights movement gave way to black power, about the bitter teachers' strike in New York City that pitted blacks against white teachers, about the deaths of the Kennedys and Martin Luther King Jr., about the deteriorating economy and the frightening rise in crime, about Ronald Reagan.

All of which is certainly true enough, but I think it's more than that. These last ten years or so have also given rise to the bizarre notion that the ability to express one's basest biases and fears—the ones once regarded as unspeakable—equals not only freedom but style. If you feel uncomfortable around blacks, if you think Italians are greaseballs, hell, don't worry about it, get a laugh with it. Nigger? Kike? They're only words. People who initially blanched at jokes involving ethnic stereotypes, even some of those who protested, soon found themselves repeating them; as a species, we are startlingly adaptable.

Nor, of course, is this curious brand of candor restricted to one's own circle of friends. Don Rickles may issue a pious disclaimer at the end of every show—"You know I only kid you; we're all God's children; I love you all"—but it follows so potent a barrage of ethnic put-downs that it leaves one's senses reeling.

"Oh, come on," retorted Jeffrey. "You're making much too big a deal over this. These are *jokes* we're talking about. They don't hurt anyone."

"Some do, some don't, perhaps it's worth making the distinction. Would you tell your Empire State joke to a black person?"

He smiled. "Of course not. The muthah might cut me up." He paused. "Okay, okay. The problem is, it's hard to see what's wrong with it when some nightclub comic is making a million bucks a year doing the same thing."

What's wrong with it, besides the fact that it reflects our own smallness of character, is that slowly, over a period of years, the jokes take on a credibility of their own. As far as millions of people in this country are concerned, Poles *are* dumber than the rest of us, Jews *are* pushier, and blacks *are* more menacing. It is much easier not to deal with someone as an individual once he has been reduced to a cliché.

It is one of the melancholy facts of life that virtually all of us harbor some degree of prejudice. But if we accept the premise that this does not reflect the best in ourselves, then we should not give in to it so readily, should certainly not glory in it, should, perhaps, even try to change it.

All of this I said to Jeffrey Stillman, and all of it he took in with equanimity. "You sound," he said with a laugh, "like all those jerks at *The Village Voice.*"

That was every bit as hard for me to take as he'd known it would be. Self righteousness may have its place—Woodrow Wilson did reasonably well with it—but all in all it is an obnoxious trait. In Jeffrey's eyes—and in mine—the humorless slug had long been at least as objectionable as whatever it is he was railing against.

"Do you know," I replied finally, in self defense, "the definition of Jewish foreplay?"

"No—what?"

"Three hours of pleading."

But, even before he'd finished laughing, I was mad at myself. "At least those jerks at *The Village Voice,*" I heard myself snapping, "care about something."

The Rape of the Lock

Some people yearn for beach houses in Acapulco or Malibu. Some lust after Maseratis or Porsches or '58 Corvettes. Me, I'm dying to get my hands on a lock of hair from the head of Andrew Jackson.

I have had this admittedly curious fixation for some years now, ever since the host at a posh dinner party I attended showed me *his* Jackson lock. Oh, this guy had snips of other people's hair in his collection also—Teddy Roosevelt's and Marilyn Monroe's come immediately to mind—but it was Andrew Jackson's hair that most intrigued me. I've always been a Jackson buff anyway, ever since he cut such a dashingly ornery figure in the Davy Crockett TV series, and here before me, silvery as the moon, was an actual little piece of him.

And then, years later, I had a chance to get one of my own. There it was, listed on page 24 of the catalog issued by Charles Hamilton Galleries, the auction house: "133 (JACKSON, ANDREW) Copious lock of Jackson's white hair, held under glass in a handsome old gilt locket of the period. . . . The locket is quite ornate, engraved with a floral wreath design. Fine."

Fine. I wanted that thing so badly I could cry, could already feel it in my hand, could already imagine my casual query of new acquaintances: "Guess what I got in my pocket?"

But, of course, there was the issue of money. On the basis of my observation of other Hamilton auctions, I surmised that it would probably go for several hundred dollars—not a staggering sum but, alas, more than enough to wipe out my current bank balance.

Still, that locket haunted me. How many pages of copy would I have to write for airline magazines, I wondered, to buy that hair? And, more realistically, how many sympathetic friends could I tap for a loan?

"Are you out of your mind?" demanded Larry Borton, nearly as broke as I. "Do you seriously think I'd lend you money for *that?*"

"Listen, Larry, I know it sounds silly. The thing is, this hair is a remarkable historical artifact, an actual piece of one of the greatest men this country has ever produced. Surely you can understand that."

He shook his head. "Christ, a few hundred bucks is a lot of money. I can eat for two months on that. As far as I'm concerned, it's just obscene to throw away money on any whim."

"It's not a whim. I need it."

"Listen," he said, "every time the guy got his hair cut, he probably left thousands of dollars' worth of hair just lying there on the floor."

"I wish I'd been around."

Larry's attitude was echoed by a number of other friends. They were amused, most of them, by the notion that I coveted Old Hickory's hair; what baffled, even appalled, them was what I was willing to pay for it. All the clichés about conspicuous consumption swirled up about me like newspaper pages in a windstorm. Possessions, I was solemnly reminded, do not bring happiness; a penny saved is still a penny earned. "What kind of role model," asked someone only half facetiously, "is Zsa Zsa Gabor?"

This was, I soon came to understand, a moral issue for these people. They, like me, had been raised on the logic that some kid in China would keel over if we didn't finish our lamb chop, and some little bit of this had never left them.

One of my friends had actually participated in the greatest uprising against self-indulgence in memory, having been among the 500 or so people to write an angry letter to *The New York Times* following the appearance in that august journal of a story by Craig Claiborne describing a thirty-one-dish, nine-wine French dinner he and Pierre Franey had consumed at a cost of $4,000. "How can anyone," demanded one irate letter—it might have served as a manifesto for the entire group—"reconcile this smugly decadent story and almost daily reports of worldwide hunger and starvation?"

It struck me at the time that there was enough hot air blown off during this controversy to heat New York City for a month. But I suppose all those people, self-serious as they were, did have a kind of point—as my friends had a point now. One has trouble remembering in a society like ours, a society where someone like Ramsey Clark is as easily discarded as last week's newsmagazine and someone like Rod Stewart is lionized, that the commonplaces about self-indulgence, like almost all commonplaces, are essentially valid.

There was a time, of course, long before the coming of the Reggie Bar, when people knew that without being reminded. It sounds odd now and, worse, pompous, and, worse still, vaguely reactionary, but abstract qualities like self-control and discipline were once seen as marks of character. People got along reasonably well without Betamaxes or Gucci shoes or meals accompanied by very old bottles of Château Latour. Indeed, a case can be made that in some ways people got along better.

But I fear that this is starting to sound more than just vaguely reactionary. There are, to be sure, also plausible arguments in *favor* of rampant self-indulgence, numbering, to be precise, two. First: In many cases it is enormously diverting, at least in the short run. The Playboy Mansion West has been called many things, but "boring" is seldom one of them. And second: It doesn't hurt anyone. This, in fact, is the reply that an obviously troubled Craig Claiborne made to his legion of scribbling detractors: "If the meal had not occurred, would one more mouth have been fed, one more body nourished?"

That sounded pretty good to me, so I picked up the theme for my own private war. "Who's it going to hurt," I asked, "if I spend a couple of hundred dollars on that lock of hair? It's not as if the alternative is to spend the money rescuing the boat people. Do you give *your* money to the boat people?"

It's extraordinary how quickly most people shut up when confronted with sophistic nonsense like that. Only one pal of mine, an Englishwoman named Sheridan Williams, offered a rejoinder. "Why," demanded Sheridan, "are Americans so damn literal? No one is suggesting that you take a vow of poverty and relinquish all your worldly goods. The point is to know within oneself what is important and valuable. Your willingness to spend so much for twenty or thirty strands of hair demonstrates—how shall I put it?—a decidedly decadent nature. As for the situation of the boat people—"

"The *plight* of the boat people," I cut her off irritably. "That's what those of you with your priorities in order call it."

"And a decidedly cynical nature, as well," she added. "Tell me, do you own a home computer?"

"Certainly."

"And what do you do with it?"

"What do I do with it? I play. I hack around. It helps me pay my bills."

She nodded. "It is my theory that only the most jaded among us invest in such things."

And in a strange way, she may have had a point. In a world where noble values were the norm, a world where "extravagant" would be a pejorative term instead of an admiring description, in such a world the Apple people would probably be in big trouble. So, for that matter, would sellers of used hair. For what it finally comes down to is terribly simple: Most of us turn to artifacts of steel or plastic for diversion because we achieve only limited nourishment from other people and, by extension, from commitment to larger issues.

That is not an original concept—nor is it pleasant to find oneself on the same side of the materialism question as Jerry Falwell and Dean Jones, not to mention every Hare Krishna disciple running around loose in the streets—but its essential accuracy seems beyond question.

And yet, and yet, for many of us who've grown up with "The Price Is Right" and with free Captain Midnight Flight Commander Signet Rings, courtesy of Ovaltine, any other way is almost beyond imagination; though we might acknowledge that we are schmucks for feeling as we do, material lust has settled permanently into our hearts. The most we can hope for is to cut our losses, to keep things in some perspective, to be preoccupied, if we must, with the thought of owning that country house but not obsessed by it, and, above all, not to let the lust show.

I finally decided, after much deliberation, that I would bid no more than $250 for the lock, a sum that would break me momentarily but would not put me in debt for years to come. And so on the night of the auction, I waited as the Buffalo Bill letters and the signed photos of Charles Lindbergh and the document bearing Aaron Burr's signature were sold. Finally, my lock of hair was announced. "We have a mail bid on this item," intoned the auctioneer, "of four hundred dollars. Do I hear four hundred and ten?"

My heart sank.

"I have four hundred," the auctioneer repeated. "Is there a bid from the floor?" Reflexively, on its own, my hand started to jerk upward.

"The stupid ass," hissed a distinguished-looking fellow sitting beside me, the one who'd come for a Bertrand Russell item. "Imagine spending four hundred dollars on *that.*"

My hand stopped at chest level.

"Sold to the mail bidder for four hundred dollars."

I exhaled deeply and slumped in my chair. Five minutes later I purchased item 137 for $55. It was a single strand of hair from the head of the poet John Keats.

On Not Turning the Other Cheek

In Paris a while back, I passed a long afternoon with my friend Neil Offen, who used to write sports for the *New York Post*. "You know what people kept asking me when Thurman Munson was killed?" said Neil at one point. "They kept asking me if I was broken up over it. See, Munson was with the Yankees when I was covering the team."

"Well," I asked, "were you?"

He shook his head. "Of course not. He was a son of a bitch when he was alive, he was still a son of a bitch when he was dead."

Neil went on to describe his first encounter with Munson, in the spring of 1970, when as a rookie sportswriter he approached the burly Yankee catcher on the team bus: "Kent State had just happened, and I knew that Munson had gone to the school. So I asked him his reaction to the killings. You know what he said? He said, 'They should have shot *all* the mother——!' " Neil paused. "I saw a lot of Munson after that, and he was usually surly if not downright mean. But as far as I was concerned, I didn't need to know any more about the man than I knew that first day."

The conversation moved on from there to Hubert Humphrey and the national orgy of wailing and gnashing of teeth that had accompanied his final days. Humphrey had not, of course, been a Thurman Munson; he was a fundamentally decent man, well intentioned and eminently likable, who had, alas, fallen victim to galloping ambition. "But you know something," said Neil, "I could never forgive him either. I thought the way everyone fell in love with him at the end was ludicrous."

"So did I," I agreed. "Suddenly this guy who had been self-serving for so long was being hailed as some kind of saint."

"There have been two great tests of public men during our lifetime—the McCarthy era and Vietnam—and Humphrey failed both of them," said Neil. "In the end, he should have been judged largely by those acts of equivocation. And I, for one, could never forgive him."

That is, perhaps, as good a reason as any why Neil now resides in France. On these shores, when it comes to moral lapses in keepers of the public trust, we tend to forgive and forget—mainly forget—with a frequency that suggests senility. A case can be made that this is a virtue—charity, glass houses, and all that—but I think it is something very like the opposite. Quite simply, there are times when it is *right* to remain intransigent in the defense of ideals.

Certainly as children we understood that. The textbook heroes—Lincoln, Churchill, Gandhi, et al.—were all individuals who perceived the right and stuck to it, often against desperate odds; the equivocators, the Neville Chamberlains of the world, we saw as buffoons or villains.

But it's the oddest thing: Growing older gives almost all of us the capacity to accept indecency with equanimity. It is naive, we begin to believe, to divide the world into good guys and bad guys. Everyone is expected to be at least a little bit corrupt.

No wonder, then, that the public person who makes it through the meat grinder of electoral politics with passion and principles intact is an aberration, regarded with wariness by his colleagues, unable by definition to achieve anything like a national constituency. The brilliant, waspish Wayne Morse, who paid for his early, angry opposition to Vietnam with his political life, recognized this as well as anyone. "You can't be the kind of figure I've been in politics," he said a month before his death, "and have ambitions to be President."

Of course not. For Morse's rage was profoundly unsettling, and Americans do not like to be unsettled. Especially today, in the wake of Vietnam and Watergate, we have retreated from even the hint of stridency, opting instead, by quiet consensus, for the middle ground; as there are no heroes abroad in the land, so do we find few villains.

The danger in all of this is manifest. If people are incapable of cherishing the notion that there are *some* lines that cannot be crossed, some acts that cannot be excused, they will not retain a sense of purpose.

But, of course, our national complacency is merely a reflection of the ease with which we equivocate in our own lives. How upset can we be with Hubert Humphrey's weakness when we readily express understanding for acquaintances who, in the name of self-growth, cavalierly shed longtime mates? When we overlook backstabbing among office colleagues? When, for that matter, we accept moral obtuseness in those closest to us? Behavior that in another time would have given rise to outrage and smoldering resentment is now too often shrugged off as being just the way things are.

It is thus terribly refreshing to run across individuals who, like Neil, can be provoked to enduring indignation. Another such on the record is Jimmy Breslin, the writer and beer-commercial personality who publishes a column at the end of each year naming the people who have earned his wrath during the previous twelve months. This list includes everyone from public officials to maître d's to individuals who have apparently once been friends of his. One year, I'll never forget, he had it in for someone he referred to simply and with terrible contempt as "Podhoretz' Wife"—in other, gentler words, Midge Decter, the writer—who had apparently wronged Breslin at some social function.

There is a fine line between justifiable anger and pettiness—I do not presume to estimate on which side of it Breslin more frequently falls—but the principle remains exemplary. One must take a stand, unequivocal and unswerving, against what one perceives as indecent behavior.

In my own case, on reflection, my expectations of others are clear enough to be reduced to categories:

From strangers I anticipate nothing more than courtesy (and if I don't get it, my irritation generally passes quickly). From colleagues I insist upon respect and equitable treatment. And from friends I demand not blanket approval but patience, understanding, and loyalty—all of which I offer in return. And if I am crossed, I do not forget easily.

Still, at not forgetting I am a piker. Many of the victims of the blacklist, people who were for years—in some cases permanently—denied access to their livelihoods, have never retreated an inch in their stand against former colleagues who named names before the congressional committees of that terrible era. They still walk across the street when they see one of the old enemies approaching. Those who cooperated with the committees, weighed down by thirty years of guilt, are often anxious to bind up the wounds but find themselves confronted by people who could not, constitutionally, compromise on principle, even if they wanted to. That is usually what got them into trouble in the first place.

Enduring resentment can change to debilitating bitterness, as it sometimes has in the case of blacklist victims. But that kind of thing occurs rarely. More often, the anger slowly dissipates; though we remember, we no longer despise.

A few years ago, John Henry Faulk, the brave, earthy Texan whose long fight against the blacklisters was the subject of his book *Fear on Trial,* described his reaction, in the aftermath of his historic court victory, upon running into the writer Abe Burrows: "He'd talked, named names, and every time he'd see me in a restaurant or somewhere, he'd wring my hand and blink his eyes frantically. I always felt a little unclean around him. I'd feel like puttin' my arm around him and sayin', 'Jesus Christ, don't feel so bad.' And *he* was the one who was working."

Psst!
Heard
the Latest?

A friend of mine—not a close friend, but someone I like a great deal—was recently featured in an article in a national magazine. I would have been very pleased for this person had the article been about some new book he had just written or an exciting adventure he had had on assignment. But it wasn't. The article was about the breakup of his marriage, and it spared no details. The other woman was named, and so were the other woman's husband and my friend's children. Then there were the quotes from my friend's friends, speculating on a possible reconciliation.

This was the first time I had ever encountered such a piece about someone I knew personally, and I felt most uncomfortable reading it. What business was this of mine? What business was it, for God's sake, of the whole nation's?

But, of course, I knew I was only being old-fashioned. No one is supposed to be embarrassed by anything anymore. Topics that only a couple of decades ago were close to unmentionable—the sexual appetites of public personages, the numbers printed on other people's contracts—are today discussed over lunch in office cafeterias as casually as the doings of Laverne and Shirley and the price of dog food.

Our most esteemed publications now have "people" columns, and editors of monthlies that once featured great fiction sit at meetings and solemnly discuss whether one celebrity on the cover will generate more newsstand sales than another. One daily newspaper in New York City has actually elevated rumor to the status of news, daily teasing the locals, like some kind of conscienceless sideshow barker, with fat black headlines about impending Russian invasions or rampant subway crime or Teddy Kennedy's sexual past.

I don't mean to be priggish about this. Gossip is as old as human nature, perhaps even older; I find it entirely conceivable that one Neanderthal man, hunched around the fire, might have turned to another, forced his lips into a grotesque grin, and made a guttural sound pertaining to the nocturnal habits of a certain Neanderthal woman. It is just that I yearn for the standards of the old days.

I shall never forget the morning when Freddie Messenger strode triumphantly into our eighth-grade homeroom, surveyed our vacant adolescent faces, and announced, "You ain't seen nothin' yet!"—at which point he unfurled a copy of the *National Enquirer* and held it aloft. MOTHER ROASTS BABY IN OVEN, EATS IT is my recollection of the headline.

Even when the *Enquirer* and its many imitators stopped trading exclusively in the grisly and their headlines screamed instead about pregnant movie stars or doomed romances or miracle cures for cancer or incredible beauty secrets of the famous, the mentality—the unapologetic voyeurism—remained the same. For years I had this persistent image of the creators of the scandal sheets, hideously misshapen creatures from the pages of Charles Addams, laboring in underground caverns, talking feverishly into telephones, in search of some well-known person's as yet un-exploited misery.

The question is not so much how sleaziness became respectable—a great many odd and terrible things have happened in this land since the Eisenhower years—as what its acceptance has done to us. Liz Smith, the decent and thoughtful lady who has ridden the crest of the gossip wave—and in the process, she says, made "more money than I'd ever imagined making in my life"—takes a hopeful view. In an interview last year she said, "There's only this intense interest in gossip . . . because we're not beset by anything truly serious except our own selfish serious-ness. . . . Sooner or later, though, as a society we're going to move on to more pertinent things."

God, I hope she's right. As a people, we don't need to know another thing about the private life of Ryan O'Neal and Farrah Fawcett. It would be an absolute blessing to see the word *superagent* instantly stricken from the language.

But frankly, it is difficult to believe that this daily bombardment of idiocy, this epidemic concern with the trivial, has not had a more profound impact on people. Inevitably, the junk information takes on a legitimacy all its own. If John Travolta is accorded forty times as much press as François Mitterand, it is altogether natural that he would be of infinitely greater concern to most people in this land. If Teddy Kennedy's romantic history is a matter of continual speculation in the press, while virtually no attention is paid to his positions on health care or arms limitation or equal opportunity, obviously he will be judged on that basis.

But it has touched us in an even more insidious way, this legitimization of the petty, for quietly—so quietly almost no one has noticed—it has insinuated its way into our personal lives. Societal pollution moves on little cat feet.

There are those for whom open displays of gratuitous nastiness are now a good deal less embarrassing than showing up at a chic party with a fleck of dandruff on the shoulder. One film executive of my acquaintance regularly calls "story conferences," the sole purpose of which is to create, and arrange for the dissemination of, reports damaging to rival executives.

But we need not dwell on extreme manifestations of the phenomenon. I know other people, individuals who a decade ago were unfailingly gracious, who sauntered into the Eighties with dispositions not unlike that of *Taxi's* Louie. It is not that they have become cruel, these people; they have simply learned that backbiting is the coin of the social realm. So they tell tales out of school: prattling on about others' relationships, or even their own; belittling the professional performance of co-workers; or, for any of a thousand reasons, referring to people whom they basically like in less than flattering terms.

The trouble with all of this, of course, aside from the fundamental fact that it is ugly behavior, is that generally the person being offered the dirt is as loose-lipped as the source himself, and the speed with which the secret information makes its way back to the target can be astonishing.

Indeed, sometimes a middleman is not even required. One fellow I know, an inveterate bigmouth, recently had an experience he describes as "the gossip's nightmare." There he was, riding with a companion on the crosstown bus, offering his low estimation of the looks, intelligence, and breath of a co-worker, announcing that the co-worker had made his way in the company only as the result of his marriage to the boss's niece, "a real airhead herself, by the way," when he chanced to glance up—right into the eyes of the airhead.

Even in its most innocuous form, talking behind someone's back often comes to no good. A friend I'll call Lois, the kind of person who worries for a week that she might have been impolite to a salesgirl, reports with despair that she has lost, perhaps forever, one of her closest friends because of a remark she chanced to make to a mutual acquaintance. "All I said," she whines, "is that I didn't think it would last between her and her boyfriend because he's a little"—she swallows hard—"obnoxious."

I try to console her. "There's nothing to feel guilty about, Lois, you just said what you thought."

She nods. "Obnoxious," she repeats, "and also a bit of an underachiever."

"An underachiever?"

"What I mean to say is that the poor fellow is never going to earn a living. She'll be supporting him forever."

Clearly the safest course, as well as the honorable one, is not to trade in cheap prattle at all. "Loose lips sink ships," went the wartime warning, and, aside from those cashing in on it, gossip hasn't done anyone a damn bit of good since.

But maybe one must be burned, severely burned, before that lesson takes hold. I remember with stunning clarity the instant when I finally got the point. It was two years ago, at a discreet literary party. For some time I had been feuding, long distance, with an editor under whom I had once worked: I would hear from friends still in the office that he had been badmouthing me; I, in turn, would say something vicious about him—which would reach his ears two days later. Thus our quarrel, which had begun as a tiny thing, escalated to a fever pitch. On the occasion in question

I was standing at the bar, quietly finishing off a drink, when suddenly my enemy, whom I had not seen in person for fifteen months, was beside me, glowering.

"Why do you hate me?" he demanded, barely able to control his rage.

"I don't hate you," I stammered.

"You've been going around telling everyone you know that you hate me. I want to know why."

I was aware that the party had grown silent around us and that thirty people were staring in our direction. "You've said the same thing about me."

"No, I haven't," he said.

"I haven't said it either."

"Don't give me that crap. I've heard it from five people."

When I get extremely nervous, I have a habit of reaching into my glass and popping an ice cube into my mouth. I reached for one now.

"Hey," I said, "let's not kid ourselves. We've both been saying lousy things about each other. Maybe we both ought to think about cutting it out."

But he wasn't listening. "Your hand," he said frigidly, in what remains the single most miserable moment of my life, "is in my drink."

Choosing
Among Evils

A while back, on assignment for a magazine, I found myself talking about American politicians with Oriana Fallaci, the volatile Italian journalist. Fallaci, as individuals from Kissinger to Khomeini have discovered, does not mince words: "A couple of years ago, I was at an embassy party in Washington, and I happened to speak with several congressmen and senators. It almost made me faint! In comparison, Italian congressmen are all Einsteins and Shakespeares. *Mamma mia!*"

To many of us, this is no startling revelation. The gaffes of our public servants are legend. Former governor Kneip of South Dakota, a Carter appointee as ambassador to Singapore, let it be known that he had never heard of Gandhi. Virginia ex-senator William Scott, accused by a small magazine of being the dumbest of congressmen, called a press conference to deny the charge. Nebraska ex-senator Roman Hruska, during the Carswell confirmation fight, commented that "There are a lot of mediocre judges and people and lawyers, and they are entitled to a little representation."

Ignorance, shortsightedness, and provincialism are not

limited to those politicians who also happen to suffer from foot-in-mouth disease. Perish the thought. In 1968, *Esquire* ran a remarkable survey of the members of Congress. Each of the 174 statesmen who responded was asked six questions, among them what his favorite film was, who his preferred writer and artist were, and what ideas or individuals had most influenced his political philosophy.

The responses to these innocent queries would boggle even so cynical a mind as Fallaci's. No fewer than thirty-two senators and congressmen named *Gone with the Wind* as their preferred film, closely followed by *Dr. Zhivago* and *The Sound of Music.* Howard Baker, who chose Ernest "Hemmingway" as his literary ideal, was one of twenty-one congressmen who misspelled the name of their favorite author, artist, or composer. Among the ideas and thinkers who had influenced our nation's leaders: a slew of fathers and grandfathers, membership in the Mormon Church, the presidential prayer breakfast, the two-party system, and "political science and congressional colleagues." All in all, a staggering portrait.

I know of not a single political reporter who would venture the opinion that today's bunch down in Washington, the ones currently gearing up for the new cold war, is any more impressive. Leafing through the pages of that old *Esquire,* I see many who remain very much on the scene, older and not wiser. Indeed, most of those few who gave the 1968 Congress any class at all—Fulbright, Gruening, Morse, Mansfield—have long since departed, many in principled defeat.

But, of course, that is the way it has always been in American politics. As a people, we have produced as distinguished a group of big-time losers—from Henry Clay to

Bob La Follette to Henry Wallace and Adlai Stevenson—as any electorate on earth. Abraham Lincoln himself could never have hoped to be voted in by all the people, his election to the presidency (with a 40-percent plurality) coming as the result of the freak circumstance of having had three strong and ideologically compatible candidates arrayed against him.

Over the long run, this can be disheartening to the point of debilitation. "I have been voting in elections since 1964," complains one friend of mine, "and not a single person I have voted for with enthusiasm has been elected. Not one. Not even to state office!"

My friend offers this by way of explanation. He has, he recently announced, simply decided to stop voting.

If he follows through, his protest will simply be lost in the shuffle. As we are informed every couple of years in postelection analyses and editorials, the majority of eligible Americans do not exercise their franchise. The word that seems to crop up most often in these mournful postmortems is "apathy." Voting is good; apathy is the enemy.

This is an assessment that some of us question. "The fact is," as my friend the new nonvoter puts it, "democracy in this country doesn't work, and it doesn't work because there are already too many ill-informed people voting. Politicians are able to push buttons: They make noise about 'Communism' or 'military preparedness' or 'busing,' and hundreds of thousands of voters follow like lambs to the slaughter. When people don't even know enough to vote their own self-interest, the system can't function smoothly."

As a solution, this fellow, whimsical in his despair, proposes that all potential voters be administered an examination. "It wouldn't be a literacy test of any kind," he says. "It would be uniform and discriminate against no one. Its purpose, quite simply, would be to separate the informed from the ill-informed. Potential voters might be asked to name the leaders of France and Britain and five Supreme Court justices, for example, and to explain the provisions of the First Amendment. These are all things that anyone helping to elect the most powerful figure in the world should be aware of, wouldn't you agree?"

On the face of it, such a notion strikes us Americans, shot through with civics-class idealism, as something like heresy, but it turns out to be a difficult proposition to argue against in practical terms. Over dinner recently, I watched my friend dismiss with a wave of the hand someone's angry argument about suffrage being an inalienable right. "Nonsense," he said. "You've got to take a test to drive a car or to be admitted to a decent college. Isn't electing a decent government just as important?"

"Goddamn it," riposted the other guest, "this is not what the Founding Fathers intended!"

"It is *precisely* what they intended. They were after a meritocracy—which is why they limited the franchise to those who owned land. In 1790, land ownership pretty much equaled a knowledge of public affairs. That limited, thoughtful electorate is why the early leadership of the country was so effective. Things only went haywire with the introduction of extended suffrage. *That's* when we got the Millard Fillmores and the Franklin Pierces!"

To add weight to his position, my friend calls upon Gore Vidal, as astute in his observation of American history as he is reportedly effective at cutting up opponents at dinner parties. In his novel *1876*, Vidal has Mark Twain, reeling after three old-fashioneds, offer his assessment of the nation's politicians: "They are all crooks—and why? Because of universal suffrage. . . . How, I ask you, can you have any kind of country when every idiot male of twenty-one or more can vote?"

But in the end, such an attitude does us less than no good, for the intractable truth is that there will not soon be any fundamental change in this country's political system. This leaves many of us precisely where we began: utterly frustrated, our choices seemingly limited to supporting candidates for whom we have no respect or to supporting no one at all.

A decade or so ago, such a choice was a lot less difficult to make. Black and white was the ideological fashion of the Vietnam era, and many of us wore our purity as casually as our jeans and work shirts. During the 1968 presidential race, which pitted Richard Nixon and George Wallace against a Hubert Humphrey whose ethical credentials had been badly sullied by four years of cheerleading for the war and an apparent insensitivity to the horrors of Chicago, we opted by the hundreds of thousands to sit it out. "Screw him" was our attitude, and screw him we did.

Well, of course, we've never heard the end of that one—of how *we* must accept a measure of responsibility for the Burger Court and "benign neglect" and five more years of Vietnam; of how, in the final analysis, we'd been jerks, a legion of political eight-year-olds throwing a tantrum.

And in a cockeyed, uniquely American kind of way, people who think that way are right. Even some of those who were bitterest in 1968, even some of us who will never entirely forgive Humphrey, now concede that politics in this country *is* largely a matter of cutting losses. Maybe it is as naive to expect candor and originality of thought in our politicians as it once was to stick daisies in rifle barrels and name children "Dandelion." Maybe the choices we get are all we should hope for.

Certainly, a great many people have come to no good hoping for more. Indeed, a reasonable case can be made that the desperate, manic self-involvement of the Seventies was little more than a pell-mell retreat from that earlier era of inflexible commitment: from SDS to est in one long, harrowing step.

But that may be the crux of our problem right there: In the same way that we expect happiness in exchange for a few hundred bucks and a couple of weekends in a locked room, so we continue to look for instant political gratification. The postwar generations—especially those of us who knew all along that we would be going on to college and white-collar lives—never learned to work for what we wanted. For many of us, perseverance remains a faintly amusing concept, like industry or steadfastness or staunchness, traits that seem somehow out-of-date.

Which is why I was faintly amused to find myself one recent evening, on assignment, at a meeting of my neighborhood political reform organization. "I'll bet," said my companion, eyeing the studious, concerned, mostly middle-aged faces around us, "there's a higher concentration in this room of people who go to Eastern European movies than in any other room in the country."

But it didn't take me long, as I watched them in action, debating issue after issue—on how to protect local merchants from the encroachments of real estate speculators, on how to elicit more federal funds for mass transit, on which of several doomed candidacies to support—to feel stirrings of real admiration for them. These were the people who had been working all along, through the bad years and into the somewhat less bad. While we'd gone about the glorious business of occupying buildings and issuing "non-negotiable demands," they were the ones who'd gone door to door, election after election, in the service of my beliefs.

At the end of the meeting, as the political reformers adjourned to the back of the room for coffee and fond talk of Adlai Stevenson, I was surpised to see an old acquaintance from my college days. He too had been involved in what we liked to call the movement—not as a leader, but he'd done more than his share of angry yelling—and we fell into easy conversation. After a few minutes, I broached the question: "Tell me, how did you end up in this place?"

He smiled faintly. "I'm here because of all the slogans from the old days, there's only one that continues to make sense to me: 'If you're not part of the solution, you're part of the problem.' "

Just
Good Friends

This is a piece about friendship, its obligations and its exigencies. It is not an easy piece to write. For although a great deal has been said and written on the subject, it seems to me that the currency of friendship is in flux. The qualities upon which relationships have always been based—mutual respect, a shared perspective, and, above all, trust—often seem no longer to come sharply into play. People brush up against one another, on the job or at leisure, and *bang!* they identify one another as friends.

What they mean, of course, is *acquaintances,* but there is more than a semantic distinction. I know people, ranging in age from their early twenties to their late sixties, who have no genuine friends whatsoever but do not know it. They socialize regularly, they *know* people, and it seems to them that this is what it is all about. In my mind's eye, the Rat Pack—Sinatra, Martin, Lawford, Davis Jr., Bishop—always epitomized this syndrome. I could be wrong, of course, but I imagine them sitting around and boozing and topping one another's jokes, and then going off and not thinking about one another for six months.

It is not an original notion that we are in the midst of an epidemic breakdown of relations between the sexes;

we've all heard more than enough about the divorce rate. But the fact that the quality of other kinds of relationships has also changed is rarely remarked upon. There are no statistics for promises broken or for confidences betrayed or—more to the point—for amical first meetings that fail to blossom into friendships at all. We are increasingly a society dedicated not so much to consumption (as the common wisdom has it) as to convenience. Since any relationship of value demands concentration and the recognition of another person's needs, it is by definition inconvenient. Thus, individuals who once might have nurtured enduring friendships during long, slow evenings full of talk now pass their evenings on their own, by the television set.

There was a time when separation used to add a new dimension to friendships, the exchange of letters revealing quirks or charms or insights never grasped face-to-face; the state of human relations has deteriorated so obviously in this regard that it *can* be measured in government reports. According to the Postal Service and trade sources, about 80 percent of today's first class mail is business-related, and of the remaining 20 percent, fully 17 percent is given over to greeting cards and other expressions of sentiment by proxy. And, of course, even most of those who do occasionally put pen to paper rarely manage more than a postcard.

To be sure, our alienated age has also seen some shifts that give reason for hope. Friendships between men and women are a good deal more common than they were even a decade ago. Indeed—and this part is not encouraging—I know several men who maintain that their dealings with other men are so habitually marked by undercurrents of hostility that they feel truly at ease *only* with their women friends.

But such men usually continue to go through the motions of friendship with those they are never quite able to be honest with. They go to dinner with them, or to the movies or to a party, and are always secretly relieved when the evening is over. A friendship—the genuine article—has nothing to do with how much or how little time is spent in each other's company. At its best, it is deeply nourishing; at its worst, it is almost as painful as the point of low ebb with a lover. But it is never static, because it presumes honesty and, very often, taking risks—saying unpleasant things because they cannot go unsaid, even acting in ways likely to offend.

At a recent dinner party, I found myself sitting beside a fellow, the director of a small company, with a problem. He had, he said, just been asked by a close friend to write a recommendation on her behalf for a job she badly covets; but he doesn't think she's qualified for it.

"What do I do?" he wondered aloud. "If I write what I feel, obviously I'll cost Joan the job." He paused. "On the other hand, who knows? Maybe I'm wrong; maybe she'd do a terrific job. As a friend, don't I owe her the opportunity to try?"

"I don't see the problem," remarked the guy opposite, genuinely perplexed. "Of course, write her the silly recommendation. What are friends for?"

Which would, I suppose, be the reaction of most of us to such a dilemma. Back scratching has become a way of life in these United States, as pervasive as fast food, as accepted as the ethnic joke. I am told by an acquaintance that the president of his firm recently installed an unqualified boyhood friend—known on the premises as "the heir transparent"—as an executive vice-president; I know a journalist who, despite the fact that her prose is devoid of wit, insight, and punctuation, now shares the by-line on magazine stories written by her boyfriend. Though most of us still prefer to speak of friendship in terms of sharing and helping, it is, clearly, increasingly a matter of having and getting more. "Of course I've made some friends with an eye toward what they could do for me," a writer I know recently remarked. "And now that I'm successful, I've stopped seeing most of them. I know that sounds lousy, but hell, that's the way the world works."

It is indeed, which is one reason the world is such an endlessly disheartening place. But the thing is, in one way or another that kind of behavior ultimately catches up with people. Sometimes, gratifyingly, it simply blows up in their faces. Warren Harding packed his White House with poker-playing cronies—and ended up one of the jackasses of history; after years of sucking up to a famous director, a political reporter of my acquaintance finally quit his job to write a screenplay for his buddy—and wound up broke and jobless.

But even in those cases in which there is no dramatic denouement, the principal players pay a price under the table. The simple fact is that it is close to impossible to engage in bogus friendships part of the time and to live with real ones the rest of the time. It is something like claiming to be in love on weekdays while heading for singles bars after work every Friday: some kinds of behavior truly are mutually exclusive.

Which is why, ultimately, the guy with the letter-of-recommendation problem called his friend and outlined his quandary. He would, he said, certainly not write a negative letter—would, if she wished, set down precisely what she dictated—but he preferred to write nothing at all. She was hurt, naturally, and the wound took a month or two to heal, but eventually the friendship prospered anew.

That is a minor example, but a telling one—in its way reminiscent of the old commercial in which one friend felt obliged to tell another that she had body odor. I used to sneer at that commercial, until someone I know told me that she had found herself in the identical situation: She had a friend, she explained, with the most god-awful BO imaginable, the kind that clears rooms, and she was faced with the choice of advising this person to bathe a bit more frequently or simply not inviting her to a sedate birthday party she was throwing. She chose the latter course, and they haven't spoken since.

That is probably as it should be, for the relationship was clearly of limited value to both of them. If people who claim to be friends have trouble discussing mundane matters, it is hard to imagine the magnitude of the silence—and the mounting frustration on both sides—that will come crowding in with an issue of consequence.

In the course of poking about for this essay, I had a long conversation with a writer whom I'll call Adam about his friendship with another writer, whom I'll call Max. I knew neither of these people especially well, but I had always liked them; both were good-humored and apparently thoughtful, and they had been best friends for years. So I was more than a little surprised to be told that they had stopped speaking to each other.

"How in the world did that happen?" I asked.

Adam shook his head. "It's complicated," he said. "How do you explain a friendship?"

"But obviously you guys have a lot in common."

He distractedly stirred his drink. "In many ways our

values are the same," he said. "I remember we once tried to pin down exactly what it was we both found so exhilarating about sports, and we concluded that it was the only aspect of American life where connections or bullshit could do someone absolutely no good. A film editor can patch up a rotten acting job, a book editor can salvage a rotten book, but there's no helping out a batter staring at Ron Guidry, or some poor schmo who's been assigned to guard Kareem. Max pointed out that Mickey Mantle's son had failed to make it as a professional ballplayer; there was a real poignancy to that, of course, but we both thought there was something nice about it, too."

"So," I pressed, "what happened between you two?"

"Well, maybe there was really less in common than met the eye," he said, laughing softly. "It began to seem to me that there was a real contradiction between what Max said and how he acted. After all the talk about being irritated by people who got ahead for the wrong reasons, it seemed to me that he did a hell of a lot of ass-kissing himself. After all the talk about the importance of being supportive, I began to find him so competitive about work that it got to be more and more unpleasant to raise the subject with him at all.

"Of course, he was having problems with me, too," Adam continued. "Apparently he was finding me more and more judgmental—something he thinks even a good friend has no right to be.

"But neither of us really knew how bad the other felt until about a week ago. The silences between us had become so intolerable that one day I took him to lunch and told him, point by point, precisely what I was feeling. And then he did the same." He paused. "It was very distressing, this confrontation, and I think we both felt a very deep sense of loss mixed with the relief. But in the end there was no animosity. We decided that since we obviously made each other feel bad, it just made sense not to see each other, at least for a while."

And that is pretty much where Adam left it. But three days later I received an envelope addressed in his hand. It held a Xerox of a note he had apparently just received, forwarded without comment:

> Adam:
>
> I care more than ever about our friendship, because for all its intermittent tensions it is obvious that there is something very worthwhile underneath. In time I know it will get better on the surface, too: the tensions will recede and the strengths will prevail, and in the meantime the time off will be for the better.
>
> Thanks for caring enough to put yourself on the line.
>
> —Max

Thy Neighbor's Life

By coincidence, the very day I heard that my friend Alex had sold his novel to the movies for several hundred thousand dollars, I had lunch with my friend Gary, who had just sold his nonfiction book to a paperback publisher for $40,000. Gary, who had never before made so much as $10,000 on a project, was ebullient—until he heard about Alex, at which news he began to choke on his quiche. "All that money for *that?*" he finally managed to say. He shook his head. "Christ, why doesn't something like that ever happen to me?"

"Damn right," said I, feeling less guilty about having dampened my companion's spirits than about being not at all displeased. "Let's face it, the world's not a fair place."

Ours is, of course, a business particularly susceptible to the rigors of galloping envy. Virtually every writer I know is jealous of someone else. Magazine writers are jealous of TV writers, TV writers of movie writers, movie writers of novelists, novelists of other novelists. Judith Krantz is undoubtedly jealous of Thomas Pynchon; Thomas Pynchon, like the rest of us, is probably jealous of Judith Krantz.

But then, lawyers I know are also envious of other

lawyers who have better practices or more attractive mates or larger summer houses, and businessmen are envious of other businessmen, and ballplayers are envious of other ball-players. I once knew a clown with a small circus who privately berated a friend who wore *his* funny nose for Ringling Bros. A convincing case can be made that the entire free enterprise system is fueled by envy.

Which is one reason why there are so many ulcers in this once-bountiful land. No emotion is so corrosive of the system and the soul as acute envy. Unlike hatred or lust or violent anger, it is internalized, and there is nothing therapeutic about it. Envying someone causes the object of envy no inconvenience whatsoever—indeed, he is likely to be gratified by the envy of others; but for the envier, envy can be debilitating to the point of paralysis.

And then there is the ugliness factor. Envy not only promotes a slew of our baser traits—gratuitous nastiness, petulance, backbiting—but generally calls them forth in an embarrassingly public fashion. Invariably we end up looking as terribly small as we feel. It is damn near impossible to envy with style; even if we offer congratulations, even if we manage praise, it somehow always comes off as grudging.

And yet, even in a volume about ethics, certain melancholy facts must be faced: Envy appears to be a permanent fixture of the human condition, persistent as memory, intractable as the head cold. In my days as a scribbler, I have passed a distressingly large number of minutes leafing through such books as Bartlett's *Familiar Quotations* and anthologies with such titles as *Great Thinkers of Western Civilization,* resenting the hell out of guys like Euripides, Milton, and Shakespeare for writing snappier, wiser lines than mine. But, I am pleased to note, even they had no special insights on the subject. Someone named Philip James Bailey put the obvious perhaps most fetchingly— "Envy's a coal comes hissing hot from hell"—but even he was a few thousand years late. In the *Apocrypha,* for God's sake, there's a remark about how "envy and wrath shorten life"—and back then the average life expectancy was only about thirty years to start with!

But if envy appears to be an integral part of the human character, it also seems clear that it thrives particularly well in certain social climes. There is comparatively little jealousy in those situations in which people adhere to common beliefs or are obliged to work together for mutual ends; many World War II veterans think back with fondness on their days in uniform precisely because, for the only time in their lives, they had felt utterly at one with those around them. The same sense of unity of purpose was also manifest on the home front during that period, although it showed itself less dramatically. With mutual goals and common vision, there was, quite simply, less room in the American soul for pettiness.

But, of course, very nearly the opposite mentality now prevails in this country. A society grounded in individual achievement and self-gratification has its pluses—some people are indeed driven to extraordinary accomplishment—but it does not make for general good feeling. "We worship success," noted Anne Morrow Lindbergh on "60 Minutes"—and this is a woman who *knows*—"but we really don't like the successful. We're envious of them."

It is difficult to grow up American and *not* envy success. A hundred times a day, overtly and subtly, from the media and from those around us, we receive the message: getting, having, being able to show off what one has—that is what counts. It is like a swarming army, this value system, burying our better instincts, overwhelming our skepticism. We even go out of our way to imitate the successful, as if somehow that might fulfill us. A cousin of mine went to see *10* a few days after it opened and spent a quarter of the film snickering over Bo Derek's ludicrous hairdo, speculating on its construction and the problems involved in its upkeep; three weeks later she was saving up in order to get one herself.

But then, envy, like slavish imitation, is at base largely a matter of self-contempt—of, at the very least, intense dissatisfaction with what one is. Not that very many of those driven by envy are able to perceive that. The confirmed envier is truly persuaded that if only he had a little more money or more recognition or a more glamorous life-style, everything would work out. The notion that values must be overhauled and ways of thinking altered is too painful to be acknowledged.

Last week I got a call from a magazine writer who has recently moved to California to make her fortune writing screenplays. She has talent, this writer, and a fair number of connections, and chances are excellent that she will do well. But after the ritual slighting of other, more successful young writers, she abruptly became self-pitying. "Oh, God," she moaned, "I don't want to end up one of those people who writes twenty scripts in ten years and gets none of them produced!"

Now, this person has every reason to hope for professional gratification, but as I listened to her it was hard for me not to feel that her universe was desperately out of whack. The simple fact is that very few of those other writers, the ones she so vigorously envies, are themselves content. They get their screenplays produced, all right, but often as not they head home after a hard day at the studio depressed and alone, or they dash home, utterly manic, gnawed at by some vague but insistent anxiety, or they forget entirely about going home and simply head over to some chic saloon to crawl into a bottle. And yet, can any of us imagine an aspiring writer shaking her head and muttering, "I don't want to end up one of those people who gets everything she writes produced and ends up miserable?"

But, in fact, that is precisely the way this writer—like anyone else driven by the same painful compulsion—must eventually begin to think if she is ever to break out of the envy-and-self-recrimination cycle. It sounds terribly obvious and, worse, banal, but probably the only thing truly worth envying is peace of mind. And that comes as a result of nothing more exotic than having values and adhering to them and not wasting time worrying about what other people do with their lives.

Without that commitment to values, even headlong flight from the source of the anxieties is likely to be of only limited comfort. Just a few days ago, in the course of mulling over this essay, I had a lengthy conversation with another writer friend, a fellow recently returned from several years in France. Prior to his departure, this person had been as competitive as anyone I know; but now, a self-described new man, he offered an ode to the healing qualities of expatriation. "The problem all along," he explained, "was being in an atmosphere that brought out the worst in me. At first, after I left this country, it was like going through withdrawal; I missed not only Johnny Carson and good delicatessen and baseball but the feeling that something important was going on around me. That is what this society had done to me: It had left me believing that nothing that happened anywhere else really mattered. It took a good eight months before I began to understand that, in fact, French politics was a good deal more interesting than American politics, that *Le Monde* was better than any American paper, that rugby is one hell of a game. And, more than that, I learned that French writers of my age envied other French writers as intensely as I'd always envied certain Americans; and to an outsider it looked completely loony. Finally I picked up some perspective. And so I stopped being tormented by my rivals' success. In fact, I stopped reading their stuff altogether, started reading the classics instead, writers whose talent dwarfed all the guys I'd always been jealous of." He reflected a moment. "I can't tell you how good it felt to stop caring about the dwarfs."

He said all of this with impressive earnestness, and it was difficult not to believe him. But then, just yesterday, leafing through my new Bartlett's, I ran across something Thomas Hobbes said way back in 1651: "The praise of ancient authors proceeds not from reverence of the dead, but from the competition and mutual envy of the living."

The Curse of Right and Wrong

I've been thinking about Walter Mondale. Here we have a man who was once among the Senate's most passionate and intractable liberals but who in four years as vice president became an entirely new public person, a preacher (in *New York Times*ese) of the "gospel of fiscal restraint and military preparedness." And grinning all the while. Fritz Mondale, in Eugene McCarthy's memorable phrase, is a fellow with the *soul* of a Vice-President.

But I've also been thinking about Gene McCarthy. McCarthy's soul may be many things, but vice-presidential has certainly never been one of them. When, in the wake of Hubert Humphrey's nomination in Chicago in 1968, McCarthy was being urged to mount the podium and make his peace with the candidate for the party's future and his own, he instead visited the battered antiwar demonstrators in Lincoln Park and welcomed them "to the government of the people in exile." And he never won elective office again.

Perhaps someone will write a book about McCarthy a century from now (if anyone is still reading) and that episode in Chicago will be remembered as heroic. We have always had a thing for martyrs in this country. From Nathan Hale to the boys at the Alamo to all of JFK's *Profiles in Courage,* those who have looked past expediency have always held a special place in the popular imagination, and the fiercer the flames that enveloped them the better we've liked it.

But it's a curious thing: Those of us who like to think that we have learned history's lessons—who try in our daily lives to abide by the same principles of dignity and decency that seem to have inspired those individuals, who will not stab others in the back or kiss ass or commit small dishonesties in the cause of self-promotion—invariably pay a price for our high-mindedness. This is a fact that we find as endlessly baffling as it is painful. Life, as we came to understand it as children, simply shouldn't work this way. "Why is it," plaintively asks a writer I know, "that so many rotten people get ahead? Do you really have to be amoral to succeed?"

The answer is that it helps a lot. And acting ethically, in and of itself, doesn't. In the real world, the meek generally earn $15,000 a year and never get their names in the papers.

If we were nobler souls, or if we lived in a society in which conventional success was less highly prized and character much more so (if we were, say, Tibetan), such awful inequities would not be quite so grating. But we're not, and they *are.* "I remember," said a close friend's mother, a woman in her late sixties, "how shocked I was by the treatment of the American veterans of the Spanish Civil War on their return to this country. Here were these incredibly principled young men who on their own had gone off to fight for the Spanish Republic and had borne unimaginable hardships; some of their units had taken ninety-percent casualties. And when they got back, not only did they get no credit, but many of them were harassed for having been premature anti-Fascists. That was the phrase: *premature anti-Fascists.*" She shook her head. "I'll tell you something: knowing right from wrong is a curse."

And yet there are those who maintain that the issue isn't nearly so simple. For a year now I have been quarreling—sometimes good-naturedly, sometimes with frank hostility—with a fellow who has, to my mind, very much too often appeared to pander to his superiors. What I find particularly disagreeable is that, while others do the same thing unconsciously, he does it calculatedly and without apparent qualms. "I happen not to regard that kind of *flexibility* as a good thing," I sneered. He gazed at me levelly. "You talk about flexibility as if it were a dirty word," he said. "It's not. But in any case the operative word for me is *complexity.* I don't see things in terms of right and wrong or good and bad; the world for me is all grays, and I apologize to no one." He paused. "I admire the purity of the other way," he said, "but I also know how to recognize self-destructive behavior."

This fellow has known me for a number of years, and he knows how to zing me as well as he knows how to snore at night. The fact of the matter is, I myself have frequently made choices in the name of ethical purity and have paid the price. There is, for example, at least one important publication for which I am no longer welcome to write, as the result of a memorable run-in with its editor. This editor is much disliked in journalistic circles, and were I to recount the incident in detail you would probably agree that I was in the right, but my pal M. Gris would certainly argue that that is beside the point. After all, dozens and dozens of other writers find it within themselves to work for this jerk; and what, in the end, do they lose by it?

Such an argument does, alas, give me pause. I have, in the past, endlessly maintained that by refusing to bend even a little I have protected my most precious resource, my self-respect. And indeed I have. But, I begin to wonder, is self-respect so fragile that it demands that degree of vigilance? And then, too, what is the ultimate cost of such missionary zeal? McCarthy will almost certainly end up a historical cipher; Mondale might yet be President.

There is, in the end, a wisp-thin line between what constitutes thoughtful behavior—behavior consistent with one's principles—and what constitutes self-righteousness for its own sake. One should never lose sight of that line. I will continue to maintain till the cows come home that I was correct in breaking with that editor, but neither should one hold oneself up as an ethical paradigm. "Everyone," notes my friend's mother, the one cursed with insight, "does what he has to do."

It must also be acknowledged that frequently those of us who excessively trumpet our own decency and rail against those we perceive to be our ethical inferiors do so out of motives that are less than pure. When one is frustrated or bitter or terrified of putting oneself on the line, virtue is never its own reward. It becomes a small solace to portray oneself as having been too principled to succeed—a convenient gambit in a society where, in fact, principles often *are* an obstacle to success. But in the end, martyrdom makes for a most unsatisfying career.

Of course, there are battles to be fought—there are many of them—but they should be judiciously chosen. Not every slight justifies a rejoinder; not every irritation need become an incident; not every fool one runs across need be informed of the fact. *Pliability* should probably be a dirty word, but *flexibility?* I suppose not.

For the sorry truth is that in this most pragmatic land, the purist is generally his own worst enemy.

A couple of months ago, I passed a weekend in the country in the company of a charming man in his late eighties who, late on Saturday evening, after many glasses of red wine, began talking about his forty-seven-year-old son, an extraordinarily gifted research physicist who has never come close to achieving the success that once seemed assured. "My son," said the old man wistfully, "is totally incapable of compromise. If a thing is so in his mind, it's like a mathematical formula; there's no other answer. He never got his doctorate because he thought it would be a betrayal of principle to stick a Ph.D. after his name the way all the other muckamucks did. He once worked for a corporation that had a dress code, and he quit over *that.*" The father paused, reflecting on his own disappointment and on his boy's bitterness, only now becoming apparent. "Why?" he asked. "After all is said and done, what was the point?"

Careless Love

This is a piece about loving and lovers, but it begins
with an incident about friendship. It begins that way because ultimately, after all the songs and movies, after all the
articles in the women's magazines and sentimental novels, it
is love and friendship that go together like a horse and
carriage.

Okay, the incident.

Andy was as morose as I had ever seen him. He had,
he explained, recently learned that his ex-wife, the woman
he professed to love still, had moved in with someone else.

"Do you know the guy?" I asked.

He nodded. "Dull," he said. "Dull as John Davidson
on an off day." He shook his head miserably. "How could
she go to *him* after *me*?"

Theirs had, in fact, been a marriage characterized by
incessant battling, one of those pairings in which neither
partner seemed capable of bending a millimeter. Indeed, to
an outsider, the love—and it had once been enormous—had
seemed to vanish within the first year.

"Have you spoken to her?" I asked.

"Yesterday."

"And?"

"I told her exactly what I thought," he said. "I told her
it was typical of her to be attracted by superficial qualities. I
told her it reminded me of all the self-destructive things

she'd done while we were together. You know what she replied?" He laughed mirthlessly. "She said she was with him precisely *because* he never said things like that."

Andy paused, genuine confusion clouding his face. "What the hell did that mean? Was what I said really so horrible?"

That, as I reflected on it afterward, was what was so intriguing about the conversation—not Andy's behavior but his utter unawareness of the resentment it would provoke. Indeed, on the basis of this single episode one might reasonably conclude that I was dealing with a lout of heroic insensitivity.

Except that Andy happens not to be that at all. He is a generous, thoughtful fellow, the kind who makes a point of befriending new people at work and who, in all the important ways, keeps old friendships warm. Indeed, I've never known him to act badly in any relationship—except the one with his wife.

But, in fact, I do not think such a situation is at all unusual. It is not big news that we in this society tend to treat strangers with cavalier disregard. Well, the sorry truth is that often we treat those to whom we are supposedly closest—our wives, husbands, lovers—most callously of all.

Which is, I suppose, something like observing that the economy isn't in terrific shape—a melancholy fact so obvious that it no longer need be remarked upon. We all understand, without ever discussing it, the real meaning behind the divorce statistics; we realize that all the standard explanations for why relationships fail—financial insecurity and sexual incompatibility and divergent interests—are just code words for the fact that people who once adored each other have simply stopped treating each other very well.

We understand that because we identify with the tendency. We know how tempting it is to lash out at a loved one after a trying day at work; we know how unspeakably irritating it can be to have an observation—or, worse, a joke—misunderstood; we realize how quickly an innocuous tiff can turn cruel. We are so accustomed to such things that we forget that it needn't be that way at all.

The actress Lynn Fontanne credited the success of her half-century collaboration, onstage and in life, with Alfred Lunt to the fact that they had never been impolite toward each other.

Well, that, finally, is what it is all about. Almost all the rest of us go through life being downright rude to one another; not constantly, of course—sometimes not even very often—but almost always often enough to take a toll. Relationships don't collapse under sledgehammer blows; they are chipped away with rubber mallets.

The spirits and egos of our lovers are as fragile as the contents of any china shop, yet almost all of us are emotional bulls. That is not to suggest that we destroy out of any malice aforethought. When asked, all of us profess to wish for nothing so dearly as the kind of relationship that will enable both parties to grow and flourish. But we rarely consider the awesome responsibilities such a union entails. Indeed, it is altogether proper these days—fashionable even—to wish, as well, for a situation in which one is guaranteed what is known as one's own space.

Well, it just won't work, because those two wishes are close to incompatible. Being overly preoccupied with self invariably means forgetting about being polite, turning thoughtless—or, simply, tuning out the other person altogether. "It was the TV that finally got to me," says a woman I know who recently fled an eight-year relationship.

"I just couldn't compete with it anymore. I'd want to talk to him, *need* to, and I'd get the back of his head. Do you know how horrible it feels to know you're less interesting than what's on television?"

What had happened to the TV watcher is what happens to so many of us: He'd gotten lazy. If familiarity is allowed to breed indifference, indifference will breed, if not contempt, then surely alienation. At that point the process is very nearly irreversible, every day becoming, in Stephen Sondheim's memorable phrase, a little death.

So profound does the alienation in such a relationship often become that even the principals themselves sometimes have difficulty recognizing their slide toward the abyss. A startling number of people must be confronted with a mate's demand for separation before they are able to acknowledge that there might be something fundamentally wrong between them. I have, on more than one occasion, seen people continue to insist even after such a demand that the problem was merely a temporary aberration. It often takes a calamity to enable us to understand clearly the mess that our insensitivity has gotten us into.

To a large degree, the sense of detachment that each of us brings to his personal life is merely an adaptation to the world at large. We are so inured to the clamor that surrounds us day to day, and we have, above all, become so indifferent to the suffering of others, that in the end we have difficulty recognizing even our own pain.

Which is another reason why living out the alternative to the dismal status quo—that is, understanding *before the fact* the likely repercussions of our behavior toward those we care about and acting upon those insights—is so agonizingly difficult. For doing so means more than simply not being gratuitously hurtful. It implies making a profound effort to be attentive; to hear not merely a lover's words but themes and subthemes; to give weight to feelings that might be logically dismissed; to be, even if one is not quite in the mood, a very good friend.

That is, of course, a kind of effort more readily accepted in the abstract. Indeed, each of us must learn a lot of hard lessons on his own before he is ready to make such an effort. And perhaps, given how frighteningly at ease we are with insensitivity, we must be prepared to relearn those lessons with some regularity.

I relearned a few myself only recently. The woman I love and I had, for several weeks, been not so much quarreling with as ignoring each other. Both of us were preoccupied with professional problems, and we had, in our own ways, made it clear that we were far more interested in what was going on in our own lives than in each other's. We were both angry and, in some unspoken way, out for retribution.

But I didn't discover where matters really stood until one summer afternoon in the country. My friend had been a track star in high school, and I was no slouch with a sneaker either, so I tauntingly challenged her to a footrace, her two laps to my three.

We began at opposite ends of the yard, and at the signal we took off. It was not until we were within ten feet, both moving at full speed, that it became clear that we were going to collide—that, in fact, we were engaged in a game of human chicken—and by then it was too late. The impact was awful; both of us collapsed to the ground, and for five minutes we writhed in agony, she clutching her rib cage, I my knee. But at last she looked at me and managed a small smile. "Hey," she said, "let's talk about it."

Shooting
an Elephant

When I was nine or ten, there was a pseudojoke that made the rounds of kiddom. The joke was not intended to get a laugh—it was not, in fact, funny—but to gauge the character of the poor schmo who was hearing it for the first time. The victim would be surrounded by four or five other kids, and someone would say, "Hey, Andy, you heard the one about the elephants in the bathtub?" This was the signal for the conspirators to begin tittering. "You'll love this, Andy." And so the joke would be told, slowly, the plotters' anticipation building with every syllable: "There are these two elephants in a bathtub, a mother elephant and a father elephant. And the mother elephant says, 'Please pass the soap.' Well, the father elephant looks at her and says, 'No soap radio!' "

At that the entire group would collapse in absolute paroxysms of laughter, almost always joined, after a confused moment, by the victim. Then, abruptly, the laughter would cease. "Why are you laughing?" someone would ask him.

"At the joke," he'd say, though of course there would already be a glint of panic in his eye.

"It's not funny, stupid. We just wanted to see if you would laugh because everyone else did."

And half an hour later the joke would be told to someone else, the former victim joining the tormentors.

This kind of thing—and there were many, many similar episodes—used to set me to thinking about how tough it was to be a kid; about how unsure of ourselves we were, about how we would do almost anything for peer approval. It was, I thought, another good reason to be in a hurry to grow up.

But, Christ, was I wrong! It turns out that, in a dozen tiny ways, we in this society fall for the elephant gag every day. What other explanation can there be for High-Tech or for hundred-dollar running suits? "Ten years ago," notes a friend of mine who works for a magazine in midtown Manhattan, "I'd ride my old three-speed Rudge to the office, and all these young businessmen and businesswomen would laugh at me. Now they're all riding bikes to work themselves. Of course, theirs all have ten speeds."

Of course.

I do not mean to suggest that conformity, or going along to get along, is a new phenomenon. Shakespeare had a hell of a lot to say on the subject. And so did Chaucer. And so—perhaps more wickedly than anyone else—did Molière, whose *bourgeois gentilhomme* tried desperately to make his way into society via lessons in dance and philosophy and whose *malade imaginaire* stooped to feigning illness in order to bring a doctor into the family.

But, of course, in this sphere as in others, the French, those sheep in nicely cut clothing, have always been particularly easy targets. Back in 1767, Benjamin Franklin, writing home from his first trip to Paris, took a potshot at the locals, marveling over that season's fashion affected by "Actresses on the Stage thro all Ranks of Ladies": a huge blot of rouge in the middle of the face.

Nor have things changed much over there since. Five years ago, the Paris magazine for which I worked ran a semifacetious piece listing our notion of what was "in" and "out" that season, with categories as diverse as children's names, soaps, publications, and political positions. I subsequently heard that a great many Parisians had stuck the article on their bathroom walls for easy reference.

But we in this country have always thought of ourselves as different. Professedly democratic, we preferred to identify with Franklin's sly skepticism. While Europeans might lionize fops and dandies, we honored the likes of Thoreau, Lincoln, and Twain. Having no emperors in our past, we prided ourselves on not being preoccupied with their new clothes.

Yet now, a century later, capitalism in full flower having spawned a huge middle class and an advertising industry to exploit it, the pursuit of status has become very nearly universal. Keeping up with the Joneses once meant owning an appropriately large home and a late-model car; today, often as not, it means having a Betamax and drinking Perrier and wearing designer jeans. In ten years it will certainly mean something else. But what it will never stop meaning for those caught up in the syndrome is that their self-worth is dictated from without; that, just like the kids who broke up over "No soap radio," they are faking it.

If we were talking here merely about styles of dress or modes of recreation, all this would be less bothersome than it is. But, in fact, being in fashion often means thinking in prescribed ways. Sometimes this is simply a matter of slavish popular devotion to the dictates of powerful institutions. It has long been a fact of theater life that certain plays stand or fall solely on the say-so of *The New York Times*.

The Museum of Modern Art enjoys similar sway in its realm, a fact endlessly irritating to those aware of the maneuvering behind the imperious facade. Artist Larry Rivers reports that a favorite painting of his hangs at MOMA only some of the time because "the current curator at the museum isn't so crazy about me. . . . You can go absolutely out of your mind trying to keep up with the shifting tastes and the crazy politics." But almost everyone who does go believes beyond question that everything hanging on the museum's walls is by definition great art.

If popular taste is easily manipulated, so too is popular opinion. Certain beliefs are deemed proper in this country, certain others improper; and though one can be transformed into the other with stunning alacrity when the government and the media arrange it—as it was arranged a decade or so ago for us to fall back in love with the Chinese—very few dare tread unescorted on unauthorized territories.

Even the heralded protests of the Sixties were, finally, very much a matter of peer pressure. I remember being immensely gratified to discover how easy it was to persuade other students at the small college I attended to declare themselves against the war—even to get them to demonstrate in the streets, marching and chanting slogans—until I understood how quickly they could be persuaded to do something else.

Then there is the no-nuke crusade. Without examining its merits—and they are considerable—it is obvious that it is marked by a staggering degree of know-nothingism. Even so uncritical an observer as Marjoe Gortner, who interviewed antinuke protesters outside the Seabrook facility for a television show, reported that he was startled by their ignorance: "Those kids knew they were supposed to be against nuclear power, but they had no idea why." That statement is, of course, close to redundant: they are no-nuke precisely because, in the wake of Three Mile Island and *The China Syndrome,* and the solemn declarations of a variety of media figures, they were supposed to be.

God forbid you should dare, in certain circles, to express enthusiasm for nuclear energy. As likely as not, you would be hooted down as quickly as a fellow of my acquaintance was recently when, having read a *Playboy* interview with William Shockley, he attempted at a dinner party to generate a conversation on Shockley's unsettling theories. "Though what Shockley had said was pretty awful," said my friend, "he'd presented well-ordered arguments, and I was eager to hear how these people would refute them. But the subject was completely taboo. It was almost as if they were afraid of it."

He had, I think, stumbled upon the operative word. So unaccustomed are most people in this society to thinking critically, on their own—so fearful are they of appearing foolish—that when challenged they reflexively retreat to banalities or to silence. It is, I think, no coincidence that speech patterns themselves have subtly changed in recent years to provide incessant reassurance to those venturing forth into the dangerous world of conversation. "I'm driving my car, right?" someone might say, obliging the listener to offer that he is, in fact, interested.

"Yeah."

"And I'm heading downtown, you know?"

"Uh huh."

"And this cop suddenly gives me a ticket, you know what I mean?"

"For sure."

The alternative to perpetually finding oneself in such conversations is as obvious as it is difficult to abide by: to understand that the only opinions and feelings worth owning up to are one's own, arrived at independently; to know, finally, that living one's life with secondhand values is like hardly living at all.

No soap radio? What the hell does *that* mean?

Looking Hard
at
Number One

My friend had a problem. Indeed, it so agitated him—so utterly dominated him—that he was unable to eat the scrambled eggs he had ordered; instead, he kept building and rebuilding them into larger and smaller piles.

The problem, as he explained it, was not an uncommon one: He was neck deep into a relationship, and he thought, especially when he was feeling guilty, that he wanted out. The woman in question was absolutely terrific—bright, supportive, attractive, endlessly decent—but all that only deepened his dilemma. His problem, finally, was that she *needed* him so much more than he needed her. Here he was, in his late thirties a hugely successful executive, the kind who routinely jets off to business meetings in Europe and is constantly juggling eight transactions in his mind; and there was she, at thirty not yet having a professional identity, still living on a trust fund. "There's just too much pressure," he said miserably. "I can't take it. What can I say? That's just the way I am."

But he had, it seemed, little reason for apology. If, in fact, the obligations he had been asked to assume were nearly as burdensome as he implied, flight was the logical recourse. No one can be faulted for chafing under the weight of the full responsibility for another person's emotional well-being.

Three weeks later I had lunch with the woman in question. She is as appealing as reported, and she makes no secret of her vulnerability. But I was not at all surprised to discover that her version of the liaison differed considerably from the one I'd already heard. "I *didn't* put pressure on him," she insisted. "God, the guy made his terror of commitment so very clear from the beginning that I bent over backward *not* to demand too much of his time, not to expect him to give too much. But was it wrong to expect something?" She paused and picked at her sliver of pecan pie, all she had ordered for lunch; she is not eating any better these days than he is. "Listen," she said, "it's not as if he made no demands himself. I was supposed to be available at all times, when he wanted, where he wanted me."

She shook her head. "The final straw was when my grandmother was in town for a visit," she said. "I hadn't seen him in a week, so when he called, I switched my plans around, had my own grandmother go to the theater with a friend so that we could have a quiet dinner together. And then, at the last minute, he canceled—precisely because he thought the evening had come to signify too much to me." She paused, and suddenly there was anger in her eyes. "What total horseshit!"

Obviously, she had a point. The kind of fear of emotional responsibility she was describing—and it is, of course, pervasive in this society, particularly among men—is as infuriating as it is frustrating. What this woman has come to realize is that the odds of a relationship's working with such a person are about the same as those of my Mets' coming back next season to take it all. No matter how much one might fervently wish for such an outcome, one is seriously advised not to bet on it.

Riding home on the bus after this second conversation, reflecting on yet another impossible romance, I thought back upon a bit of dialogue from *Fiddler on the Roof*. Tevye, caught in the middle of a quarrel between two friends, observes that first one and then the other is absolutely right. "How," demands someone else, "can they both be right?" Tevye thinks that over for just a moment before responding, "You know, you're also right."

Well, the apparent truth was that both my friend and his star-crossed lover were right: It is, I think, a toss-up as to whether it's more difficult to sustain a relationship with a person seeking to build a world on someone else's back or with one whose back caves in at the merest hint of pressure. If one accepts the proposition—and I do—that the relationships most likely to prosper are those between relative equals, with each partner ready to give solace and share responsibility, then the unhappy fact would appear to be that neither of these thoroughly decent people is in for a smooth ride.

But what I found particularly poignant about their predicament was that, although the magnitude of the problem of each was as clear to an outsider as it was galling to the other partner, neither protagonist had faced it himself or herself. To be sure, each paid lip service to the notion that the other had a kind of point—there were even a few mea culpas—but there appeared to be no visceral acceptance of responsibility. As far as each seemed to be concerned, all it would take was a light behavioral adjustment or perhaps a wee bit more caution, and the next time around things would work out just dandy.

Thus do self-destructive patterns repeat themselves.

Nor, I think, was this situation out of the ordinary. Despite all the talk in this society of "growth" and "consciousness," despite entire movements dedicated to the proposition that people are clamoring to face up to their deficiencies, despite the fact that in the varied history of civilization, never has there been a people so wholly preoccupied with its own emotional well-being, very few of us are actually ready to look honestly at ourselves. We all have within us a thousand ways to avoid unpalatable truths, countless cul-de-sacs of the heart and mind. When we are unloved, it is because others are callous; when we are incapable of love, others are unlovable; we will be glib about our problems, or impervious or maudlin, but almost never will we be utterly straight with ourselves.

And that being that, all our efforts to make ourselves happy (the most abused word in the English language) will invariably end up as emotional tap dancing, noisy motion leading absolutely nowhere. The truth is, most of us don't know and don't want to know.

There are, of course, good reasons for that—almost all of them having to do with self-defense. Almost all of us are, in one way or another, confused or alienated or quietly desperate, and the notion of rummaging about looking for answers is terrifying. I know of one woman, the mother of a friend, who is erratic to a highly unsettling degree; indeed, she has produced a brood of children now in their twenties and thirties who are still reeling from her motherly ministrations. But this woman is as utterly incapable of acknowledging that there might be something amiss in her makeup as is a garrulous television wrestler of admitting self-doubt in the pre-match interview. Like my star-crossed friends, she has found her way of surviving in the world, and though it is more often for the worse than for the better, she is not about to change.

No more daring are the vast majority of those who subscribe so readily to the self-awareness industry. Now that the "me" boom is apparently subsiding and the economy is at front and center, we are confronted by a landscape littered with hundreds of thousands of bewildered souls—veterans of est or TM or Silva Mind Control or all three—still trying to decide how to feel better about themselves; wondering, perhaps, with Jerry Rubin, if inner peace might finally be found in the fold of a nice paycheck. In the land of the ready solution and the glib response, almost anyone can be king.

Those devoted to more traditional kinds of therapy have tended to regard the newer, slicker, mass-oriented forms of treatment with the disdain of physicians for salesmen of snake oil; they quite properly recognize that promises of "fast, fast, fast relief" are ludicrous even in TV commercials. But all too often even psychotherapy proves a useless, albeit comforting, indulgence. I have one friend, herself a former therapist, who flatly maintains that treatment almost never results in fundamental change. The operative concept, as far as she is concerned, is "adjustment" —a kind of turning of knobs aimed at producing an individual who can avoid the real issues. "Most people come in for treatment," she says, "to feel good about themselves. Basically, they just want to be told that what they're doing is okay, so they can keep on doing it. Real change involves enormous pain; that's why I have such immense respect for those who actually work toward it. But most people are not looking for change. They're after confirmation."

Our capacity for self-delusion and self-justification is unfettered by reason, perspective, or insight. In my experience, the individual most utterly immune to self-understanding is a fellow who, in looking at others, is strikingly realistic. He will offer a concise, deadly accurate appraisal of a friend's emotional state, examining its antecedents, both personal and cultural, and then will turn around and offer explanations straight out of Mother Goose for his own behavior. While everyone else is best served, in his eyes, by acknowledging basic needs and striving to meet them, he—unable to commit himself or to open himself up to others—insists on trying to cast his own life as a romantic idyll and himself as a character in a Paco Rabanne ad. The contrast is so vivid it can be funny—he will, in confident moments, laugh at himself—but finally, of course, it is sad.

There is, obviously, no task more difficult for any of us than to begin to close the gap between what we are and what we fervently wish to be, but there is also none more worth undertaking. Alas, there is no formula for how to go about it, no course in which one can enroll, no guru to be hunted down for ready solutions. Each of us must, on his own, simply start with questions: Why do I keep dodging commitment? Why don't I have greater self-esteem? Why did I do that to him? To her? To myself? Why the endless anxieties or the abrupt swings of mood? What the hell is going on?

The answers are often hard to absorb, for they lead to other, more profound questions. But it is the only process that will produce results, the only one that will strip away defensiveness so that we may, at long last, begin to read ourselves as nonfiction.

No one said it was going to be easy, but hey, who wants to go on tap dancing forever?

To Breed
or Not
to Breed

Some time ago, *New York* magazine published an article entitled "The Mid-Life Maternity Blues," about the quandary of childless women in their thirties. This is a fascinating subject; moreover, the author is a close friend; but that is not what prompted my enormous interest in the piece. No, I was eager to read the article, had anticipated it for weeks, because I suspected—more than suspected—that it would include one specific bit of information.

And sure enough, there it was, right up near the beginning of the piece. There was the woman I live with explaining our abortion: " 'I do want to have children eventually,' she said, 'but not yet. First we want a chance to spend some time together alone. A baby at this point would be intrusive.' "

It had been a lot more complicated than that, of course, and so much more agonizing that the smoothest writer in the world could never have hoped to capture it in a single paragraph: the talk and the tears; the self-doubts and doubts about each other; the way she looked at me when, against every instinct, she finally determined to go ahead with it; the sight of her immediately afterward—drawn, with a desperately anxious look in her eye; the weeks of silent anger and guilt; the way we very nearly came apart over it.

It was an utterly excruciating time, but we had at last learned the melancholy lesson that hundreds of thousands of others who like to think of themselves as progressive had learned before us: that abortion cannot be viewed exclusively, or even primarily, as a political issue. The decision to abort, even when it seems the only reasonable option, is a deeply disturbing one. Indeed, it may be as good a measure of our generation as any that so many men and women in their twenties or thirties, whose biological alarm clocks should be blasting away at full volume, *do* make that decision to abort so blithely.

"Alice is pregnant," a guy at my gym confided to me a few weeks ago, with what is a fairly common attitude and one not limited to men. "I'm taking her for an abortion on Thursday."

"Oh, Christ, that's awful," I said.

He shrugged. "It's not the first time," he said, smiling, "and probably not the last."

I am nearly as startled by the seeming ease with which other couples, unforced by circumstances, determine that they never intend to have children at all, that childlessness is simply too blissful a state to mess around with. The explanations proffered for such an attitude have become commonplace—career demands, financial considerations, the constrictions on time and life-style that children impose—but the regularity with which these explanations are repeated does not make them any less bloodless. In the end, the conclusion seems inescapable: we postwar kids, the most indulged youngsters in the history of the planet, have grown into the most profoundly selfish generation of adults.

I am not suggesting that there is intrinsic merit in those who breed. God knows there are already more than enough people who have had children thoughtlessly or for the wrong reasons—producing offspring is, after all, at the moment enjoying a certain vogue—and that is the ghastliest, the most irresponsible, the most irrevocable mistake of all. An acquaintance of mine who runs a nursery school reports that the children who pass through her classroom these days are visibly more needful than those she saw fifteen years ago: "A frightening number of these children—three- and four-year-olds, from middle and upper-middle class homes—are absolutely desperate for love. Their parents are simply too involved in their own lives to bother with them in any kind of systematic way." She paused. "I'm telling you, there should be a law that you can't have a kid unless you've gone to school and gotten a degree in parenting."

In the best of all possible children's worlds—a world ruled by Buffalo Bob and administered by Mister Rogers—there probably would be such a law. But in the world as we find it, a staggering amount of responsibility is thrust, unasked for, upon each of us. And each of us should be measured, finally, by how he handles it.

This is not a didactic essay; I do not intend to enumerate rights and wrongs. The decision whether or not to have children is among the most profound any of us will make in our lives, and when we make it, nobody's values should matter except one's own. But we are a society given to ease, to the glib response, and to the efficient solution, and if we continue to deal with the issue of having children as cavalierly as we do so much else, we will, in fact, be mortgaging our future. However each of us acts upon this question, it is incumbent upon him to understand precisely what he is doing and why, and to accept full responsibility for the consequences.

Taking responsibility has, of course, become one of the

grossly overused terms of the age, but never is it more legitimate than in this context. New parents, if they are conscientious, must be prepared to deal not only with this strange, frighteningly helpless creature who is suddenly in their midst but with elements of themselves that had been safely hidden away. "The world is a terribly painful place," noted a friend of mine, a West Coast child psychologist, "and most people spend their lives not facing up to their own vulnerability. Well, a baby is the literal personification of vulnerability. It's no wonder so many people flee that responsibility."

Indeed, so many of us have fled so diligently that we find it impossible to imagine taking such responsibility at all. "It is absolutely staggering to me," says one twenty-nine-year-old woman of my acquaintance, "to think that my mother had three kids by the time she was my age. I can't imagine myself with even one."

Nor is it surprising, given the general mind-set of our generation, that even some of those who have become parents regard the state with distaste. Another friend of mine, a writer named David Black, reported that when he and his wife announced that they were to have a baby, virtually everything he heard, even from people with children, was cautionary. "After a while I began to see it myself as something that would be onerous and a burden," he said. "Everyone said it would *ruin* things—our sex life, our time together, my work. Well, it didn't. In fact, there's so much that's absolutely, unutterably joyful about it, the trade-off is overwhelmingly positive."

David paused for a long moment. "The issue here is growing up—not in the sense of acting mature in the eyes of the adults, but of growing up morally. Before our daughter,

Susannah, was born, I could not conceive of giving up my life for another person. Writing was the most important thing to me—including my wife, Debby; including myself. But now there's no question I would give up my life for Susannah. And now I'd also give up my life for Debby. The process is actually altruistic."

Verbal pyrotechnics aside, that, it seems to me, is the thing so many of us have forgotten. Remembering it—or, more precisely, relearning it—can be terrifying, for it involves taking profound risks. But then, emotional growth, the real thing, almost always is. That, too, is a trade-off.

But I am afraid I have not been wholly honest here. This piece was not entirely precipitated by the *New York* magazine article, or even by my own experiences with abortion. A few days ago the woman I live with—she will be my wife by the time this appears—called, breathless, to announce that, yes, she was pregnant again. I find myself by turns elated, morose, and scared to death.

We're thinking of "Sadie" for a girl.

Ah, Sweet Vengeance!

Martha had a plan. In circumstances like these, Martha always had a plan. Her friend Jake, a minor executive at the New York office of a film studio, had been maneuvered out of a promotion by an ambition-consumed rival, and Martha damn well wasn't about to take it sitting down.

"Here's what we do," she said, leaning forward conspiratorially, though the restaurant was empty except for the five of us at the table. "We're gonna make a total fool out of the guy. We're gonna make him the laughingstock of the industry."

Jake grinned. "I could go for that," he said.

"How?" I asked.

Martha drummed her fingers on the table. "It's complicated," she said. "We're going to need some help out on the Coast, but I think I know where to get it." And then she presented the plan, a caper rivaling that of *The Sting* in scope. A few days hence, the rival would receive a call from an actor friend of Martha's posing as an important executive at Twentieth Century-Fox in California. The friend would hint at a job offer and urge him to drop everything in New York and come to California the next day. This important executive would add, casually, that the rival should fly out first class, register at the Beverly Hills Hotel, and drop the receipts off with his secretary when he arrived for the meeting. Then—this was the beauty part—another pal of Martha's, who worked as a secretary at the studio, would make sure there would be a pass in the rival's name waiting at the gate, insuring that he would actually make his way up to the executive's office—to face the humiliation of learning that no one there had the slightest idea who he was.

"Who knows?" concluded Martha triumphantly. "With luck, his current boss will find out about it. He might even get fired!"

There followed such an eruption of good cheer around the table that a waitress was drawn over to inquire whether we might be interested in a bottle of champagne. Only one of us—Jake's wife, Susan—remained aloof from the bonhomie.

"I'd just like to ask one thing," she ventured finally. "What is all of this going to accomplish?"

The rest of us looked at her in bald astonishment. "What will it accomplish?" repeated Martha. "It will accomplish *revenge.*"

In the end, thanks to Susan's considerable powers of dissuasion, Jake refused to give the plan his go-ahead, and Martha was left more than a little disappointed. But I don't mean to convey the wrong impression about Martha. She is, in general, a lovely woman—thoughtful, courteous, and as loyal as anyone I have ever known. Indeed, that is why she lashes out with such energy at those who cross her or hers.

That impulse is understandable because it is so terribly human. Most of us have felt surges of hostility so violent, so compelling, that we have literally fantasized murder. There was a period five or six years ago—it lasted a month—when I used to lie awake at night wondering how I might do away (inconspicuously yet very, very painfully) with a particularly loathsome agent who had double-crossed me. I still have to swallow hard when I think about the creep.

Indeed, what I personally find far less comprehensible than any imagined act of violence is utter calm in the face of terrible provocation. The "don't get mad, get even" mentality, *that,* to my mind, is the reaction that truly runs counter to every healthy human impulse. The fact that it has become embraced as a philosophy, not only by the efficiency experts who direct organized crime but by legions of political leaders and chamber-of-commerce types as well, has, the case can surely be made, a very great deal to do with the unhappy state in which this society finds itself. It is not for nothing that "J.R." rings true to so many millions of us.

But, of course, Jake's wife was right. Retribution for its own sake is hardly a reasonable alternative. Almost all of Martha's small acts of revenge would appear to have been justly motivated, and some of them have even worked, but not one has succeeded in righting the initial wrong. Nor, for that matter, have they served to make Martha or her friends feel better for more than a few minutes. For, of course, they have never touched the source of the pain.

With depressing frequency, the traveler along the low road actually ends up feeling a lot worse. For starters, we *look* so irredeemably small when we're caught being vindictive. I shudder to imagine how Jake would have reacted if the California scheme had gone through and his rival or—Jesus!—his boss had chanced upon its origin.

But detection is almost beside the point. The fact is,

vindictive behavior and meanness of spirit finally make us as small as those we despise. Even when we do manage to hurt others as we have been hurt, we succeed, in a real sense, only in further victimizing ourselves.

That, obviously, is not an easy thing for one fixated on vengeance to recognize, for the impulse itself tends not only to obscure better impulses but to stymie logic. Not long ago I received a letter from a very articulate fellow who indicated that he would not rest until he saw an old girlfriend demolished as she had, two years earlier, demolished him. What, he queried in all earnestness, was the best way to achieve the goal? A confrontation of some kind? A carefully crafted series of hate letters? A public pie in the face?

There was a terrible poignancy to this note, not only because it was quite apparent that the girlfriend had, in fact, done him considerable dirt, but because he was clearly letting himself in for a great deal more pain.

But vindictive behavior can be even more destructive than that, for, of course, it often wounds those wholly apart from the initial dispute. A friend of mine tells of arriving at her office one morning to find her boss, a prominent magazine editor, in tears. "She'd recently been dumped by her husband," said my friend, "and she was absolutely shattered. But suddenly she stopped crying. 'I'm going to get even,' she announced. 'I'm going to tell our daughter how her father screwed around when I was pregnant.' And I swear to God, she meant it!"

Relatively few people would be quite that candid about their vindictive intentions, but it is a pretty good bet that the editor would not be the first on her block to have adopted such a tactic.

"I tried to get her to calm down," continued my

friend. "I explained to her how sorry she'd be later."

" 'Okay,' she replied, 'then what do you suggest I do to him?'

" 'Nothing. Just go along as best you can, and eventually you'll get past this. The best way to get back at him is to show him how well you can do without him.' "

My friend, as you might surmise, is a soul of staggering sweetness, and she continues to express dismay at her boss's reaction. The editor ordered her from the room forthwith. Like most of us, my friend's boss was so used to operating the other way—to getting slammed and getting even—that she was incapable of recognizing the elementary truth of that famous maxim: Living well *is* the best revenge.

At this juncture another, more recent, adage springs to mind: What goes around comes around. It is, all in all, a terrific sentiment, and I know a lot of people who would turn handsprings if only they could be assured it was true.

Well, I'm here to do some assuring. The fact is, the editor's husband (if he is as vicious a bastard as she maintains) will almost certainly get his, and so will Jake's rival and all of Martha's many nemeses. They might be successful professionally—might even, conceivably, seem to lead placid domestic lives—but it is almost a sure thing that all of those people are in knots inside. People at peace with themselves simply don't act cruelly toward others. When the rest of us finally accept that law of human behavior, we'll be a hell of a lot better off ourselves.

I am all too well aware that such a view of the world is easier to set down on paper than to apply to one's own experience. Just a couple of weeks ago, I laid aside the beginnings of this essay to thumb through a local magazine of some repute, and there, to my astonishment, I found a vicious attack on the character of a very close friend of mine, whose much-acclaimed first novel had recently been published. Now, I care immensely about this fellow and am familiar with the fragility of his ego, and I found myself irate on his behalf. Not only had the attack—by a supposedly reputable journalist—been needlessly vituperative, it was also, I knew, completely without foundation. When I called my friend, I discovered that he had moved from deep depression to rage and was now ready to sling a little mud himself. "What do you think," he asked, "of my getting a friend in the press to blast the son of a bitch? Or would it be better just to call his editor myself? *I want the bastard to pay.*"

So, as it happened, did I, but for the moment we decided to do nothing more dramatic than discuss it over dinner. As I was leaving for this rendezvous I got a call from another old friend, a guy just back from a long business trip, and I suggested that he join us.

This other fellow made it to the restaurant just as the novelist and I were warming to the unpleasant subject at hand. When he'd gotten an earful, he broke into a broad grin.

"What's so funny?" I demanded. "Did you read what that guy wrote?"

"Yeah, I read it."

"So what's so funny?" I asked.

He laughed. "That you two are taking it so seriously." He turned to our friend. "Don't you know about that guy?" he asked. "For years he's been trying to get someone to pay attention to his own fiction. He's the most bitter guy in town."

This last, I understood, was hyperbole—the town in

question was, after all, New York—but the revelation was more than enough to restore our friend's good humor. After eliciting a few more details about his adversary's ugly disposition, he settled back to enjoy his meal.

And enjoy it he did. By dessert he was in better spirits than I'd seen him in for months.

"No more plotting?" I inquired.

He laughed. "Nah. His private demons seem to be handling him just fine."

Oh, Grow Up!

You can bet John Lennon would have loved it.

There, one evening not long ago, on Johnny Carson's guest couch, sat Jimmy Stewart, acting like a caricature of Jimmy Stewart. Still boyish-looking, endlessly befuddled in that chipper way, he hemmed and stuttered through ten minutes of small talk, and then Carson, obviously charmed, departed from his question sheet. "Do you *feel* old?" he asked.

"Sure!"

The answer, so unexpected in its lack of equivocation, brought forth a big laugh, which seemed to baffle the actor even more. "I . . . I look in the mirror and I'm *old,*" Stewart explained.

And a moment later he went on to prove it, telling of his reaction to watching his contemporaries, their hearing gone, futilely trying to engage in conversation. "I can stand so much, and then I say"—suddenly he jerked a hearing aid from his ear—" 'Get one; they work!' "

Though the laughter-and-applause signs in the Burbank studio were surely blinking like crazy the instant the words were out of his mouth, I believe the huge audience reaction to the remark was nearly spontaneous. For there was a guilelessness to the man, and an ease with himself, that were nothing less than wonderful. We're simply not used to that kind of candor on television, certainly not on a talk show, absolutely not on the subject of aging. On a medium that has become the principal instrument for promoting the ideal of perpetual youth, the sight of an elderly person addressing himself to the subject of physical deterioration and being witty about it to boot is about as surprising as it would be to catch Michael Landon abusing a puppy. There are old people on television, all right, but whether spry or wise or just plain dotty, they are almost always cute. No one, says the wisdom of the network office, wants to face mortality after a hard day's work.

It has been frequently observed that our obsession with youth—and our extraordinary fear of losing it—are among the saddest and most destructive aberrations of this culture. One cannot despise one's sagging skin and live contentedly within it. The lengths to which those driven by obsession go—from lying about their age to having plastic surgery to leaving longtime companions for younger ones to wearing clothes that make them ridiculous—would have baffled, and almost certainly alarmed, our forbears. What, they would surely have asked, is the dishonor in age? Why the mania to join those who think young, when those who think young often don't think at all?

But in recent years, with the coming of age of the postwar generation, the preoccupation with enduring youth has taken an even more alarming turn. For, in fact, many of us in our late twenties and early thirties have adamantly refused to move past *emotional* adolescence. Forget about the inability to face what it means to be sixty or seventy or eighty; some of us can't face what it means to be thirty-two.

In the most obvious sense, that unwillingness to grow up has to do with the general and seemingly permanent attachment of our generation to the glory days of the Sixties. I know a fair number of people, some of them extremely successful, who profess not to have felt right about themselves, not for a day, during all the years since. "It's not just that anything seemed possible then," says an independent producer of my acquaintance, dredging up perhaps the oldest standard of all. "It's that we truly believed it would never end. When it did, I was devastated. I'm not kidding myself; I know that what I've been doing ever since is trying to recreate the kinds of emotional ties with people I had then."

Though he will certainly never acknowledge it, the producer has succeeded to a remarkable degree. In the last twelve or thirteen years, not one of his literally dozens of romantic liaisons has lasted more than six months. There was, you may recall, a lot of falling in and out of love in the glory days, but feelings, though intense, tended not to be terribly profound. That may be an extreme example of the phenomenon, but it is no secret that the inability to make a commitment is the social fact of the age.

Another sign of emotional adolescence is our inability to curb physically self-destructive behavior. A couple of months ago I sat in a bar in Cooperstown, New York, watching an ABC-TV report on the latest surge of heroin use in this country, an epidemic that has infected not only ghetto blacks but middle-class whites of my generation. One of the locals, a heavy guy in hunting duds, abruptly turned to me, the youngest person in the room by a good fifteen years. "Why the hell do they do those things to themselves, those people?" he demanded.

I shrugged. "Kicks," I suggested.

"C'mon, I'm serious. Don't kid around."

Who was kidding around? It may not be the most sensible behavior in the world, but we've been thoughtless for so long it's almost second nature. Before, it was speed and acid. Now it's coke and, for some, a little smack. And, of course, virtually everyone still does grass from time to time, for better sex or simply to deaden the nerves, though we know—we can feel—that with every toke we're killing off more brain cells than you can shake a stick at. "I'm not kidding around, sir." Uh uh. In the final analysis, our lack of responsibility extends even to ourselves.

And the curious thing is that we are so rarely called on it. A guy I know remarked recently that our generation is fated—because, as the babies that made the boom, there are so damn many of us—to dictate societal trends and values for decades to come. Maybe it's true. A lame biography of Jim Morrison, that lamentable wreck of a human being who became a sixties icon, actually reached number one on the trade paperback lists. Who knows, maybe we will never be called on it.

But our inability to grow up, in the fullest sense of the term, goes well beyond considerations of life-style. For the simple truth is, many of us are unable to even think of ourselves as adults. Where the generations that preceded us were obliged, by historical circumstances, or economic necessity, or the elementary expectations of the day, to assume immense responsibilities at an early age, many of us, ten and fifteen years older than they, continue to define ourselves as kids. I spent a rollicking half hour with a friend over dinner not long ago, during which we attempted to imagine how various friends and acquaintances might have performed had they been attached to a nineteenth-century wagon train heading west. (Zach complaining an hour outside of St. Joe, Missouri, that his tennis shoes pinched; Barbara worrying about what smallpox would do to her complexion; Alex insisting on ketchup with his raw prairie dog.) Around dessert, my friend broke into a wicked parody of "She's Leaving Home (Bye, Bye)."

Which brings us, in an extraordinarily circuitous way, back to John Lennon, or, more precisely, to his death. In the days following that awful evening, many of us assured each other—and it quickly became one of the principal themes of the story in the press—that the event signaled the end of our youth. We were, it seemed, mourning for ourselves as much as for Lennon himself. This was not something that struck me as inappropriate—God knows I'd done plenty of crying myself—until a friend for whom I have great respect announced that she was fed up with the whole business. "Does this mean," she demanded, "that my father's youth won't end till Frank Sinatra dies? Frankly, I don't think that anyone who goes around saying such a thing will have to worry about losing his youth for a long, long time." She paused. "When are people going to start defining themselves by what *they* do?"

The most ironic aspect of the widespread sense of personal disorientation occasioned by Lennon's death is that it was so at odds with his own view of the world. "If the Beatles or the Sixties had a message," he said in the *Playboy* interview that appeared just before his death, "it was to learn to swim. Period. And once you learn to swim, swim. The people who are hung up on the Beatles' and Sixties' dream missed the whole point when the Sixties' dream *became* the point."

In his own life, of course, Lennon was a long-distance

swimmer. His was a story of continual growth. While so many of his listeners kept on buying the adolescent values and facile notions of romance purveyed by the Beatles even in their later work, he himself became capable, over the years, of profound and enduring commitment. He learned to shrug off peer pressure and came to understand that the only answers worth having are those one learns on one's own. That, finally, is what made him so obviously at ease with himself. The tragedy of his death is not that we outsiders are no longer able to look to him as an example but that so fully functioning a human being is needlessly gone and that his wife and son will no longer have him knocking around the house.

"When I'm Sixty-Four" was, of course, one of the most memorably playful of all the Beatles' songs, and its subtext—the preposterousness of the notion that *we* might someday grow decrepit—was one that we accepted uncritically; hell, at that point many of us couldn't see thirty. It was thus interesting to note Lennon's response in the *Playboy* piece to the question on his thoughts about the song: "Paul completely. I would never even dream of writing a song like that."

Of course not. Lennon's dreams were different. According to his widow, the two of them had devised a long list of future plans. Both, she said, had assumed they would live into their eighties.

I cannot help believing that John Lennon would have made every bit as terrific an old man as Jimmy Stewart.

Between Good and Evil

One weekend last winter, in something akin to a frenzy, a guy I know named Eric sought out virtually everyone he knew to ask this question: "Do you think it's wrong for someone to buy an apartment in a converted transient hotel?"

The someone in question was, of course, Eric himself; but for those of you far from the canyons of Manhattan, the rest of it probably requires some explanation. The housing crunch in the big town has grown so severe in the past few years—and property values have risen so rapidly—that more than a few landlords, out for the big score, have gotten as nasty as anyone ever conjured up by Dickens. Owners of some of the seedy residential hotels that dot the Upper West Side of Manhattan Island have taken to trying to evict their tenants—most of them nonwhite, all of them poor— illegally, so that the buildings might be put to more profitable use: that is, renovated, converted into co-ops, and sold to those individuals who have lately come to be known, without irony, as the urban gentry.

Enter Eric. He is a fellow of instinctively humanitarian impulses, and when the reports initially appeared in the local press of said landlords in action—threatening their tenants with court action, turning off their heat and hot water, menacing them with clubs and baseball bats, sometimes even routing them from their beds at night and nailing their front doors shut behind them—he was, like much of the city, indignant. These landlords, one heard in conversation after conversation, were despicable. Something should be done to stop them.

But a housing crunch is, after all, a housing crunch, and one day, a couple of months after press attention to the issue had subsided, Eric, who had been on the prowl for a new home for weeks, stumbled upon an excellent buy—in one of the very buildings cited in the reports. "Look," he told me when he called with his question, "I feel terrible about what happened to those people. I wish them justice. I wish that, just once, people like that could do to a landlord what the Italians finally got to do to Mussolini." He paused. "But why should I suffer? Someone's going to live in that apartment; why shouldn't it be me?"

That is a luxury we in this society have long taken for granted, the freedom not to allow our ideas in general to impinge upon our feelings, or even on our actions, in particular—and to almost never be censured for the contradiction. Those regarded as political progressives are, it is well known, particularly vulnerable to the charge of hypocrisy; we have all read enough to fill a small volume about liberal senators who send their kids to private schools and about liberal cocktail parties that feature blacks in livery. American liberals, as Romain Gary put it during the early Seventies, "have got a sense of injustice bigger than anyone else, but not much of a sense of justice—that is they don't want to face the consequences."

But the inability to face the consequences of beliefs is by no means the exclusive preserve of any ideological faction. Though it might seem a good deal less arduous a task to be a consistent conservative—what is the trick, after all, in abiding by a philosophy that essentially calls for looking out for oneself?—we have repeatedly seen (in the arguments against free trade by those with a stake in domestic automobile sales; in the appeals for government subsidies by those in the nuclear-power business; in the rush of businessmen to lay claim to new markets in what, only a few years ago, they had contemptuously referred to as *Red* China) how often looking out for oneself means turning aside from abstract principle.

Some of us do not even have the good sense to be embarrassed by the distance between what we are and what we profess to be. I recall a guy at college, a well-known battler against the twin evils of war and inequity, who was challenged about accepting checks from his father, the vice-president of a company that manufactured chemical defoliants. The guy just shrugged. "Hey," he said, *"I'm* not making the stuff."

But that is probably an exception to the rule. Self-justification is a human reflex; almost all of us, caught up in the syndrome of censure and reward, at least want to appear to be doing the right thing, even when such pretenses fly in the face of the obvious. Indeed, a convincing case could probably be made that it is only peer pressure that keeps many of us as honest as we are. God only knows what we as individuals (never mind the oil companies and all those folks leaking noxious wastes into the water supply) might try to get away with if no one were watching. As a little kid, I used to ask myself what I would do if given the chance to exchange my life for all those who had died in the Holocaust. My solution to that knotty problem, after much internal debate, was that I would do it—but not anonymously. "I know exactly what you mean," exclaimed my wife when I told her about my long-ago metaphysical tug of war. "It used to astound me when I was a kid that The Millionaire would give away all that money every week without getting any credit."

That is one of the things that make children so very remarkable: how casually they ask the big questions and how unabashedly straightforward their answers are. But we learn, we learn. The process of growing up may not change our notions of right and wrong, but it certainly wreaks havoc upon our sense of the *value* of adhering to the right. In life, even more routinely than on TV, lousy behavior is rewarded while principled behavior remains its own reward. Seeing it all, day after day, year after year, one is tempted to start screaming, "Goddamn it, it wasn't supposed to be this way!"

And then we adjust.

To thrive in this society—hell, even to exist—invariably means to tolerate in oneself a certain degree of inconsistency. In a land where flexibility has come to be smiled upon as the ultimate virtue, there is precious little choice. Every time we go to the supermarket, every time we deposit money in a bank, every time we let our kids watch some garbage on TV, chances are reasonably good that we're violating some belief or other.

Of course, groups of Americans throughout our history have actually tried to live out their convictions. During the Thirties many American Communists, wide-eyed and certain, altered their daily lives in countless small ways;

I know a few old ex-Lefties who to this day have not seen *Gone with the Wind*. In the most fundamental sense, it was that rigidity—not their beliefs—that made them un-American.

From a distance (for those of us raised on Paul Muni movies and on other historical myths), that kind of zeal always looks admirable. There is, for example, something stirring in the sight of the Berrigan brothers, still, after all these years, fighting the good fight. But most of us have long since learned that only those souls harboring a resolve close to indestructible—the Martin Luther Kings, the Allard Lowensteins, the Ramsey Clarks—can long sustain that level of commitment in a climate as inhospitable to idealism as ours. We have too often seen how easily American romantics become rock-hard cynics. "Just watch," sneered a guy I know, a veteran of the civil rights movement, when I mentioned the Berrigans. "If they stay at it long enough, someone will eventually make a TV movie about them. And they'll play themselves, too!" We know, instinctively, that the surest way to avoid such surrenders to the times is for each of us to make a separate peace.

But that is very different from deserting one's sense of right and wrong. It means, rather, that in a world chock-full of small-mindedness and inequity, a world in which greed and vanity are encouraged—*promoted*—at every turn, one must choose one's battleground. Each of us should know which lines he will not cross—would not even consider crossing—both in his personal life and in the world at large, and those principles must remain inviolate.

A few years ago, following the release of *Stardust Memories,* when Woody Allen suddenly became fair game for hero reduction, there came a slew of press reports on the alleged inconsistencies of his private life. We learned that those cruddy old shirts he wears are custom-made; that, his famous longing for privacy notwithstanding, he turns up nightly at chic eateries. But as of this writing, what one has read very little about is that the man who appeared in *The Front*, alarmed by the current political climate, has been quietly working within the industry to ward off the possibility of another blacklist.

Which brings us, in a roundabout way, back to Eric and his dilemma. As I listened to him, the specifics of the welfare-hotels issue quickly became secondary. All his friends had followed the hotel-conversion story in the papers when it first broke, of course, but in the time since, we had become inured to it; it was a blight on the social landscape, to be sure, but only one of many recently—and not even the most shocking. Frankly, in the wide world of my concerns, it ranked in importance somewhere between El Salvador and Tom Seaver's upcoming season.

But, of course, because of his potential involvement, the issue had come to matter desperately to Eric—and that is what counted. Indeed, by the end of that weekend, his decision about buying the apartment had been transformed, tacitly, into a measure of his substance.

And that is why when, at long last, he put aside the self-justifications and all the facile advice and elected to keep hunting for a place to live, many of us close to him were relieved. I do not have a dictionary within reach, but I have my own definition of character. It is a pleasure to see it confirmed, however occasionally.

Success
and Its
Discontents

Rummaging through an old filing cabinet one recent afternoon, I came upon a crumpled sheet of paper labeled, in black ink, "Play-person Data Sheet." The brain raced and the eye scanned the page. Ah, yes, my very own version of the information sheet filled out by every *Playboy* Playmate of the Month. This one had been composed one rollicking evening several years ago as a girlfriend sat across the room composing hers.

Height: 5'9½"
Weight: 145
Sign: Sagittarius
Birth Date: Nov. 25, 1948/N.Y.C.
Goals: To be recognized as a major writer; to make a large amount of money; with above assets, to live comfortably in varying locales with a woman I love and a couple of children.
Turn-ons: Good wine, excellent cigars. In a love interest: brains, wit, unselfconscious sex appeal, a good heart, determination.
Turn-offs: Stupidity, undeserved success, banal

thinking, any of a dozen qualities one might associate with Tom Landry.

Favorite Performers: Harpo Marx, Jean-Pierre Léaud, Buster Keaton, Rodney Dangerfield, Louis Armstrong.

Favorite TV Shows: "Car 54," "The Honeymooners," the original "Dick Van Dyke Show."

Favorite Movies: Stolen Kisses, Rules of the Game, Alice's Restaurant, Sunday Bloody Sunday, The Producers, The Cocoanuts, High Noon.

Favorite Activies: Playing softball, interviewing in French, rummaging through interesting historical documents, antiquing.

Ideal Evening: Getting dressed up, lingering for hours over a very fine dinner—including limitless quantities of a quality wine—with four or five close friends; smoking two good cigars over tea as conversation continues; staggering back to a swank hotel room with the woman I feel closest to and screwing my brains out; falling into a sound sleep.

Special Dream: Holding high political office.

Seeing it again, reading it all with a reasonably detached eye, it struck me as pretty damn bald. A *major* writer. *High* political office. The arrogance of it, the unabashed chutzpah.

It is, alas, all true. I have never made any particular secret of my wish to make a mark with my work. When asked, this is how I put it: "When I am sixty-five or seventy, I'd like to be able to hold a book in my hands that I'm proud of." Nor is such cheek unusual in my business. It was, I think, Norman Mailer who observed what colossal arrogance it takes to put pen to paper in the first place, and to assume that anyone will care what one has to say.

As for my visions of political office (and the office, by the way, was the presidency), well, that one dates from the Kennedy era. At least a half dozen other junior high schoolers of my acquaintance—all naive and most as prohibitively Jewish as I—shared the same dream. Indeed, I am already far behind in the timetable I set for myself back then; by now I should be in the U.S. Senate, quietly plotting my run for the top spot in '88.

But, explanations or no explanations, so blatant an exhibition of high hopes for oneself always seems unbecoming. Americans tend to be curiously schizophrenic about success; though recognition is prized—and celebrity nearly worshiped—the fact of being obviously on the make is regarded as unseemly. We may be intrigued by Richard Dreyfuss, but Jimmy Stewart and Gary Cooper remain our ideals.

Indeed, diffidence seems so appealing a trait that we tend to endow those bearing it with an inherent decency. I once spent six months trying hard to get to know an awkward, mild-mannered co-worker, only to finally discover that he was among the greatest slimes I'd ever encountered; it's just that he was a *shy* slime.

And, of course, it also works very much the other way around. Several years ago, I wrote a profile of a New York politician named Andrew Stein (no relation), who at the time was in the midst of a heated campaign for the Manhattan borough presidency. Now, those of you who are glancingly familiar with Andy Stein are aware of the man's excessive immodesty, of the way he will posture for reporters at the merest hint of an opportunity, dropping quotable quotes like the Muhammad Ali of the old days. (What other local official in the land will repeat, whenever asked, that, yes, he is angling to be President?) But, in reporting the piece, I was struck by the reluctance of so many people—including a fair number of other pols—to acknowledge Stein's record on the issues. The ambition was truly *all* that they could see—though he was actually no more ambitious than most of the rest of them, only less discreet.

The truth is, if the record counts for anything, aggressive, even grasping, behavior seems to be very much an integral part of our national character. Indeed, in the minds of countless foreigners, it is the chief component of the American stereotype. The very clichés of mainstream existence—"keeping up with the Joneses," "the man in the gray flannel suit," the various sayings of Vince Lombardi—carry with them a connotation of a people incessantly pushing for more, endlessly seeking to impress. In the Sixties, when many young Americans became, in effect, enemies of their government, it was no accident that they simultaneously turned en masse against this value system.

By now, of course, the revolution itself has been institutionalized; it is the basis of a counterstereotype. "Well," writes a friend of a friend from Monterey, California, "I went ahead and quit my job at the day-care center, and now I'm taking yoga, aerobic dance, holistic healing, and improv classes. At last, a career I can get into!"

But, of course, even those more traditional in outlook frequently have trouble gearing themselves to the emotional rigors of the American working world. Women particularly—under intense, often self-imposed pressure to succeed professionally, yet unprepared by experience to run over people en route to wherever it is they think they should be heading—often find themselves in an unsettling quandary. A woman I know is a junior executive with a fashion concern; her boss, a man, has been pushing her to cozy up to important folk on behalf of the team. "Of course I'm ambitious," she protested to me, "but I don't want to become one of *those people.*"

Nor, heaven forbid, should she. It is my own strong opinion that, if at all feasible (and it is generally more feasible than we allow), one should get the hell out of a lousy work situation and into a less lousy one. I urged the junior exec, whose true passion it is to rummage through thrift and secondhand clothes shops, to open up a store of her own, or to ferret out costumes for theatrical companies, or do any like thing that will bring in sufficient income. Such work, I reassured her, is every bit as valid as what she was doing. Self-satisfaction, after all, should figure somewhere in the equation.

But, at the same time, it seems to me that ambition and aggressiveness have gotten a bad name in our time. What *is* indecent, what anyone whose values are reasonably in order *should* question, is a work situation that demands unprincipled behavior, either in day-to-day functioning or as a prerequisite for advancement. During the period when Watergate was flooding the front pages, it was frequently observed that the win-at-all-costs syndrome that had permeated the Nixon White House was merely a reflection of a mentality pervasive in all walks of American life. Obviously, there was some truth to it; most of us have, in our professional lives, run across Haldemans and Ehrlichmans, not to mention countless snivelling Magruders and Deans.

However, there are—and it is a measure of how cynical

we have become that it needs to be remarked upon—untold thousands in this country who have done very nicely for themselves without sacrificing an iota of integrity. To be sure, their progress in the world is sometimes less easily ascendant than that of those of more flexible morality. A friend told me recently about her father, a gifted teacher of physics at a large university, who in the face of nearly incontrovertible evidence to the contrary continued to insist to his family that brains alone would guarantee his rise in the department. "It took him eight more years to make professor than it should have," she says, "but the day he got the news, he brought home a cake with two words on top: YOU SEE."

The very simple truth is that ambition and integrity are no more mutually exclusive than wisdom and wit. Indeed, the impulse to succeed is ultimately what makes human beings create great works and engage in noble deeds in the first place. Our problem—and, yes, for some it is nearly insurmountable—is to get beyond the psychological flotsam that has become inextricably bound up with the idea of success in this country. It is essential for those driven to succeed to learn, and relearn, that how one gets there is finally as important as the arriving; and for those ill at ease with the whole process to understand that no one is corruptible unless he lets himself be.

I realize that these are notions that run counter to the accepted wisdom of those on both sides of the fence. "Listen," I was reminded by an unapologetically aimless fellow I have known since high school when I mentioned to him the subject of this piece, "lousy behavior has always paid off in these United States. It's an honored tradition. Look at the robber barons, and the sweatshop owners, and most of the political establishment."

But, as it happened, that very afternoon I was reminded of another tradition from our collective past. In a secondhand bookstore in lower Manhattan, between dusty volumes of Evelyn Waugh and Edith Wharton, I discovered a thin book by one Frank V. Webster entitled *Tom the Telephone Boy.* It was published in 1909 and it is the story of how Tom, through honesty, diligence, and—a wonderful forgotten word—*pluck,* outdoes an unscrupulous rival to rise from telephone operator in a law office to whiz-kid attorney. I suspect that seventy years ago it inspired little boys and girls by the score. In fact, if you read it in the right frame of mind, it's still inspiring today. Hell, it's almost enough to set a man dreaming of the presidency.

Easy Money, Easy Virtue

The other afternoon, co-op hunting in the newspaper, I ran across an ad for an apartment on the Upper West Side of Manhattan available to rent for $1,850 a month. Now the Upper West Side, though markedly more chic today than in years past, remains an essentially middle-income district, and I was thus curious to discover just what this place (which was not located at a particularly chic address) might look like.

The snappy young real-estate lady who met me in the lobby, though she would be collecting 15 percent of a year's rent for her services, had not yet seen the apartment herself. But that didn't stop her from pushing it. "What a fabulous lobby," she exclaimed as we rose in the elevator. "Did you notice the ceiling?" Then, a few floors higher: "I'm so excited! I adore these big, old apartments!"

And the apartment was indeed awfully nice, with rooms all over the place and a pretty view of Upper West Side rooftops. But my companion behaved as though we'd been afforded an inside track to paradise. "I can't believe this! How gorgeous! Look at this, you could have *four* bedrooms here. I have to tell you the truth. Frankly, I didn't expect it to be much, but this is gorgeous!" A beat. "The lady who owns it has another offer, but she doesn't like the people. Let's hurry down to the office and sign a contract."

When, withstanding a fair amount of cajoling and a little bullying, I convinced her at last that, no, I didn't think I was going to take the place, she was not at all disappointed. I stood beside her on the street while she dialed her office and barked into the phone: "Tell her not to rent it. Tell her I'll get her twenty-four hundred dollars for it."

Even in the best of times, of course, those who deal in the roofs over our heads—agents, realtors, landlords—are in many quarters regarded with suspicion. So it is perhaps courting incredulity to begin building a general case upon such an incident. However, my visit with the real-estate agent occurred toward the end of a day marked by a series of not dissimilar episodes. One acquaintance of mine, a staunch liberal, had informed me by phone, and without the merest hint of irony, that he could kick himself for having failed to buy defense stocks prior to Reagan's election. Another guy, a fine writer, had told me over lunch that on the basis of the big numbers dropped by an independent producer, he has opted to work on a film project that will, at best, be inane, and might turn out to be morally reprehensible. I had heard from another acquaintance, who was thrilled to death because his old Ford had been broadsided by a very wealthy hosiery manufacturer with expired plates. The unfortunate hosiery manufacturer was reportedly ready to pay through the nose.

This frenzied hustling after the big score has become, quite literally, inescapable. Suddenly it seems that everyone is looking to make a great deal of money in return for the least possible effort, and scruples be damned. Indeed, the truth is, the excessive greed of the lady in the big apartment had not even struck me as anomalous. Friends of mine hoping to sell their own apartments for five or six or ten times what they paid for them are hardly more admirable; nor are all those otherwise respectable citizens who a while back attached themselves so readily to pyramid schemes; nor are those anxious souls who today study the silver or commodities markets the way, in calmer times, they used to study box scores; nor are those many thousands who have guaranteed the fortunes of authors of books with titles like *The Lazy Man's Way to Riches.*

Of course, easy money and lots of it is not exactly a new addition to the catalog of human fantasies. And in this society, where from the very beginning people have been measured, and tended to measure themselves, by the bottom line, the fantasy of unearned wealth has been as persistent as hope itself. It was the impetus behind the great gold and land rushes of the last century, behind all those many thousands of quirky devices listed with the U.S. Patent Office, behind all the idol makers of show business and more than a few of the idols themselves. It is no accident that the big-money quiz shows and supermarketlike gambling casinos were born in this country.

But in the past, I think, we kept the fantasy in perspective. While as Americans it was the birthright of each of us to play Walter Mitty, we always regarded those who turned themselves inside out in pursuit of the mirage—those who actually *bought* the Brooklyn Bridge—as fools, and rather pathetic ones at that. In the end our values were very nearly consistent with those of our forbears. From the time of Miles Standish to the era of Frank Capra, the lessons had been handed down—nothing truly worthwhile comes easily;

one makes something of oneself by setting goals and working toward them; character is ultimately what counts—and for most people these values were as sound as the dollar.

In a sense they still are—which is one excellent explanation for why they have fallen so widely out of favor. "People are scared," notes a friend of mine, in self-defense, "and principles don't do terribly well in times of fear. With prices and interest and unemployment rates where they are, people aren't feeling very secure. A lot of us are ready to do whatever we have to to produce income, short of illegality—and some of us haven't excluded that."

Different today, too, is that those subscribing to the "anything for a buck" mentality have grown shamelessly brazen. What is an eleven-year-old to make of a television ad campaign for a product called Goldigger jeans that features two of his contemporaries picking up each other in a disco?

What, for that matter, is a forty-year-old to make of his government, under pressure from the infant-formula lobby, standing alone among the industrialized nations of the world in opposing a measure designed to save the lives of a million newborns annually?

And, of course, there is also the matter of rising expectations. With the incessant reports of entertainers, ballplayers, businessmen, realtors, actors, and even writers who have become, often with stunning swiftness, indecently wealthy, we have become an entire nation with its nose pressed up against the candy-store window. As my friend puts it, "People feel like fools for not getting their share." He smiles. "I'm a fool and don't I know it, but even fools can have their charms. . . ."

But the other side—how they feel, or should feel, after

a few years of assiduously playing the angles—cannot be so lightly shrugged off. The fact is that that real-estate agent seemed so intent on financial gain that she might have summoned up the Ghost of Christmas Past right there on the fourteenth floor. And the part-time fortune makers, similarly fixated on the quick score and equally ready to put aside qualms about right and wrong to achieve it, are little better.

At the time that John Lennon was killed, I was visiting a tiny upstate New York community. I will not soon forget the shock of seeing, within thirty-six hours of the murder, a young woman turn up in a diner wearing a Lennon memorial T-shirt.

That that awful event was being squeezed for dollars should not, in retrospect, have come as a surprise, not after the exploitation of so many other tragedies in recent years. Indeed, in the time since the murder, we have witnessed many, many others—from button manufacturers, to organizers of "Beatles conventions," to publishers and record company executives—cash in, in their turn. But, finally, the question must be asked: What does all of this say about us as a people? At long last, to paraphrase Joseph Welch's lament at the Army-McCarthy hearings, have we left no sense of decency?

I did not know John Lennon, but I did know Jean Seberg, and reasonably well. She was a remarkably fine human being, fragile as crystal but animated by spunk and vivid humor—in contrast to the way she has often of late been portrayed.

When I came to know her in Paris, several years before her apparent suicide, Jean was quite obviously troubled, and not just by the profound personal woes that have made grist for so many mills over the last couple of years. She was, lest we forget, an actress of some standing; but the public, particularly on this side of the water, had lost interest and the film offers had all but stopped coming. And so, in her late thirties and by no means wealthy, she found herself examining other career options. She enjoyed writing, so life behind an Olivetti seemed the way to go; indeed, at one point she broached the idea of a monthly column from Paris for *Esquire* magazine. But it was rejected, as were most of her other brave attempts to sell herself in this new guise.

The easy sell, she knew, was an autobiography. Seberg was, after all, a beauty who had had influential friends and lovers on both sides of the Atlantic; who had helped shape contemporary cinema; who had moved between the worlds of show business and politics, from glitzy stardom to bold experimentation, from state dinners to clandestine activity on behalf of revolutionaries, in a manner unique in her generation.

But it was a notion she approached with great trepidation. "My problem," she told me one evening, "is my parents. It would cause them such enormous embarrassment. I don't know, I think I'll wait. . . ."

Forget for a moment about all of those so suddenly interested in Jean Seberg. Would you, if the money were waiting on the table, let yourself be stopped by such a consideration?

Feelings
Will Out

Some months ago, very early on in my life as a father, I grievously offended a close friend of my wife's. It was a bit after eight A.M. when she called; my wife was at the laundromat and I was an hour and a half into a marathon shake-and-hug session with our irate five-week-old daughter, who was, however, prepared to cease her howling only in exchange for a ready breast. Nothing else would do. As these things go, it had been a good month since anyone in the house had gotten anything resembling a good night's sleep.

"Well," said the friend, sudden sunshine piercing a hangover, "how's the happy daddy?"

"Lousy," I replied.

There was a moment's hesitation. I do not know this woman particularly well. "Oh, c'mon," she said finally, "you don't really mean that."

"You wanna bet?"

And, of course, I did mean it, at least at that moment. But this woman, bright as she is, did not grasp that. It later got back to us, via another friend, that she thought that (a) I had been unspeakably rude to her and that (b) I did not much cotton to fatherhood.

That is something I suspect all new parents discover quickly, how general are the expectations of others of how they should feel. To wit: Tingly and warm and perpetually giddy. Indeed, any deviation from the sugar-and-spice norm is liable to be regarded not only as unfortunate but as emotionally aberrant.

Worse, far worse, one invariably begins to impose that same set of expectations on oneself. And failing to meet them, as almost everyone does, one is left feeling like the louse of the world.

I love my little girl an extraordinary amount; I have, in fact, surprised myself with my talent for fathering. The truth is, since Sadie's birth, I have been so wholly preoccupied with the minutiae of her progress—from the growth of the microscopic hairs on her bald head to the lengthening of her attention span—that I have been effectively lost to the larger world. For the first time, I have an understanding of the appeal of uninterrupted househusbandry. And, also for the first time, I know what it means to love uncritically, and without restraint.

But then too, almost from the beginning, there have been moments when I've wanted nothing more than to flee the house and hop the first plane headed anywhere. And there have been more than a few times when I've been guilt-ridden—and too quick with a hostile remark—over my sudden inability to meet work deadlines. On one occasion during the first couple of months of fatherhood, late on yet another project and finding myself in the midst of a swirling controversy over the relative merits of Huggies and Luvs, I actually heard myself announce to a stunned roomful of elderly relatives, "Who gives a damn, they both cover her ass!"

But there was considerable solace in learning that I

was hardly alone in harboring frustrations of that kind. I have discovered that virtually every recent father of my acquaintance, and the occasional new mother as well, seems to be caught up in the same syndrome: failing, to a greater or lesser degree, to live up to the ideal.

"I adore my kid," says one friend, a successful publicist, in prelude to a particularly sorry lament, "but my life is a shambles. My work is suffering, my sex life is shot, and I'm constantly irritable. But when people talk to me about the baby, they get all googly-eyed, and I'm supposed to get googly-eyed also. The only one in my house who's allowed to act the way he really feels is the kid himself." "I never thought I'd say this," says a woman I know, a designer, who, after the birth of her baby, read more child-rearing books and attended more parenting classes than I realized existed, "but I don't think I want any more children after all. The fact is, I care about my career too much."

But, of course, such sentiments are almost never for general consumption; they are, rather, acknowledged in hushed tones, the emotional equivalent of dirty postcards sold under the counter.

Men touched by such ambivalence tend to be especially guarded—because their feelings are so often (and so sharply) at odds with those of their mates, not to mention postfeminist expectations in general. For—need it even be remarked upon?—a baby signals, with stunning clarity, the putative end of life according to the Playboy Philosophy, a passage that many men regard with genuine horror. "My God," declared a guy I know recently, six months into the pregnancy his longtime girlfriend had at last prevailed upon him to accept, *"me* with a kid?" He paused, shook his head, and retreated behind an imitation of a desperate Gene Wilder in *The Producers*. "No way out, no way out . . ."

For such men, at such times, the pressure and the sense of inadequacy are literally inescapable. Indeed, even those who, in other contexts, are wholly insensible to remorse can be thus afflicted. In his autobiography, Jacques Mesrine, the most notorious French gangster of the modern era, a casual killer as feared by his criminal associates as by the authorities, expressed regret only once: for passing the evening of the birth of his daughter not at the hospital with his wife but at home in bed with a pair of prostitutes.

But I don't want to get bogged down here in talk of babies; the issue at hand—the conflict between what one is and what one is expected to be—touches almost all of us. I know a guy, for example, who suspects there is something terribly wrong with him because, alone among his siblings, he felt no impulse to cry at his mother's funeral. "On one level, I know it's ridiculous," he says. "I've read the books, I know I was only repressing. But you should have seen the way people looked at me at the funeral."

Another acquaintance, a writer as much esteemed in certain circles for his public displays of conscience as for the quality of his prose, recently found himself subject to censure, a circumstance prompted by the revelation during his divorce that he had been considerably less than a model husband. "Quite a few people were genuinely surprised," he says sadly. "They assumed that I was a better guy than I am." He pauses. "I only wish I were."

And, then, there are the untold thousands of women in this country, perhaps millions, who are permanently down on themselves because, in defiance of the latter-day rules of the game, they are simply not career-oriented. "I feel like a total schlepp," complains one such, a strikingly intelligent young woman who has held a string of dead-end jobs. "My friends are all pushing ahead professionally and everyone keeps bugging me about my plans. Every time I call my parents, they have another job strategy—I think my mother got the term out of *Working Woman*—they want me to pursue. Even the men I know seem to think I'm incomplete. It seems that no one has much use for an aspiring housewife these days."

Indeed, in a number of ways the feminist revolution, for all the eyes it's opened and all the barriers it's breached, has tended to lock individuals into modes of thought and behavior with which they are less than comfortable. Several years ago in California I witnessed a promising relationship self-destruct during the course of a two-hour car ride over the insistence of the woman involved, a person by nature as doggedly monogamous as Marabel Morgan, that (as was frequently argued at the time) since men and women have identical sex drives, she was every bit as likely to stray as her boyfriend. Convincing as this might have been in the abstract, as much as she might have wished it to be so, it simply did not jibe with the specifics of the situation. Though a member of a feminist support group, the boyfriend, who sat in uncomfortable silence throughout, had a long history of romantic infidelity, and his problem on that score was by no means resolved. But the woman, noting the skepticism of the others in the car, insisted on making her case until we were within ten miles of our destination, at which point tears welled in her eyes, she ordered the car stopped, and she stalked out.

It was probably just as well for both of them that the relationship ended soon thereafter, for their mutual inability to come clean would almost certainly have done them in anyway. The fact is, masking one's actual feelings in a bid for the esteem of others simply does not work, not over the long haul. In case after hurtful case, for example, those new fathers who persist in refusing to face their anxieties about fatherhood end up spending less and less time at home or, at best, allowing themselves to be present only physically until, finally, their bonds to their families are as tenuous as chewing gum stretched across a room.

To be sure, doing it the other way—being straightforward with oneself and with those one cares about, even when one's feelings are considerably less than noble—has its pitfalls. A good deal of what goes on in our heads and hearts, exposed to the light of day, is liable to provoke pain or outrage.

But it can also be a revelation to discover how very good it feels getting it out and how often those around us react better than we had anticipated. For the very process of being honest with someone implies a respect that is almost invariably appreciated.

I learned that lesson again just the other week. Sadie had been crying for an hour and, once again, I was behind on my work.

"How's it going?" inquired my wife, suddenly looming behind me.

"How the hell does it look like it's going?" A deep breath. "Frankly, sometimes I wish I could just snap my fingers and make the two of you disappear for a few days."

She smiled. "Done. I just got off the phone with my parents. They're expecting us on Tuesday. I'm pretty damn sick of your face, too."

I can't tell you how much better both of us felt.

The
Long Haul

My uncle Sol, who died not long ago, was, among many other things, a fierce fan of the New York Mets. Indeed, he loathed the rival teams that came face-to-face with his Metsies with a passion he otherwise reserved for anti-Semites, unreconstructed and neo.

As it happens, I too am a Mets follower, but I am considerably less ardent in my devotion; this being a two-league country, I have long given half of myself over to the Minnesota Twins.

The significance of these unremarkable facts will, I hope, become apparent in due course. But, in the meantime, an incident . . .

Late on a torrid Sunday morning in June 1965, my friend Freddy Katzenberg and I got into my father's Peugeot and hit the Hutchinson River Parkway, Yankee Stadium-bound. The two of us went to ball games with some frequency in those days, either to the Bronx or to Queens, where the Mets had lately taken up residence at Shea Stadium; but this was to be no ordinary outing. See, my Twins were in town, the suddenly (after decades of frustration) *first place* Twins. These Twins were a club built on staggering power—the names Oliva, Killebrew, Allison, and Mincher, in that order, still generate within me a rush of anticipation—and they were anchored by just enough effective starting pitching, in the persons of Camil Pascual and the young Jim Kaat, to be for real. Thus it was that on that long-ago Sunday we carried with us, neatly folded in the back seat, the twelve-foot banner I had spent the previous week creating. It read: PASCUAL AND KAAT/AND TWO DAYS OF SWAT.

To this day I flatter myself that those words might have become that memorable team's slogan had Freddy and I only had the smarts, when parading the banner through the stands between games of that day's doubleheader, to turn it toward the press box instead of the field. But at the time, public relations was the furthest thing from our minds. The mighty Twins had just taken the first contest from the despised, fading Yankees, and they were about to take the second; they were, indeed, moving inexorably toward the American League pennant and on to an October rendezvous with Sandy Koufax and the Dodgers! For me, for every Twins fan, the suffering of seasons past was at last coming to an end.

I had not, to be sure, been suffering with that ball club quite as long as some—only about eleven years. I recall, in fact, the very day my suffering began, a spring afternoon in 1965 when my father made me a gift of my first baseball glove, a Roy Sievers model. Since Sievers then roamed left field for what were often referred to as the "hapless" Washington Senators—later to move west and become the "hapless" Minnesota Twins—my fate was sealed.

So that glorious 1965 baseball season was more than just a source of enduring satisfaction; it was, in the fullest sense, a vindication. Indeed, as those similarly gratified by the triumphs of the '51 Giants or the '55 Dodgers or the '60 Pirates will certainly attest, the bad years are what gave the belated good one its extraordinary resonance.

Uncle Sol's memorable baseball year, the memorable year for all Mets fans, was, of course, 1969, when, like twenty-five fairy-tale frogs, the perpetually inept New Yorkers suddenly, inexplicably, found themselves hardball princes of the land. But—and here we are at last making a point—the joy in Metsville that accompanied that surge already seems of another era. For, like so much of professional baseball—like daytime World Series games and real grass and announcers with regional flair—the long-suffering rooter is increasingly an anachronism. Mediocre ball clubs that just a couple of decades ago would have been embraced by their communities the way Our Gang embraced their mangy mutt—with a blind eye and an irrational sense of possibility—are today likely to play to near-empty ball parks (as, in fact, have the Mets themselves in recent years), roundly dismissed with that cruelest of American epithets, "losers."

I was never one of those who bought the argument, often proffered during the Sixties, when the football boom paralleled the escalation in Vietnam, that organized sports in this country mirror our shifting sensibilities as a people. In this instance, however, there is a correlation. We are, quite simply, losing our talent for perseverance. We of the postwar generation, especially, having been raised on TV instead of books, having as adolescents been animated by soft drugs and hard music instead of ideas, have come to regard quick gratification as something like a birthright. The desultory fact is confirmed as readily in the statistics

measuring job turnover and failed marriages as in the atten-
dance figures at the bottom of any baseball box score; our
attachments tend to be superficial and transitory. We have,
many of us, learned to measure satisfaction the way itchy
television executives gauge the success of dim-witted comedies—week to week, day to day, moment to moment. We
exaggerate momentary frustrations, grossly magnify unex-
ceptional problems, routinely jettison relationships that
prove inconvenient. For some of us, the very concept of the
long haul has become as irrelevant as a George M. Cohan
lyric.

Increasingly, even our most primal ties—those to our
families—are subject to neglect, a trend well documented
(as if there were any doubt) in a recent volume entitled
Grandparents/Grandchildren, the Vital Connection. "I've
called [my children] and said 'come,'" says one grandmother cited in the book who, typically, lives within driving
distance of her family. "They say 'sure.' But they never do.
I've lost my grandchildren and they've lost me."

My Uncle Sol, like so many of his generation, could
never bring himself to accept the latter-day mores. A con-
tentious type, as famous in the family for his derisive wit as
for his generosity, he was always ready to sneer at the values of the younger set. I suspect that he in turn was regarded by most of my contemporaries who chanced across
his path as a classic fogy.

But they might well have profited by his example, for
Sol was, in his quaint, unobtrusive way, an inspiration, as
constant and undaunted in a hundred ways as he was in his
devotion to the Mets. In 1923, at twenty-one, after working his way through New York University and graduating
with high honors in chemical engineering, he learned be-

latedly that he had prepared himself for an industry that, in those days, did not hire Jews. After a degrading year and a half of turndowns, another man might have been crushed or permanently embittered; Sol simply marshaled his resources and returned to school for two more years and became a pharmacist. Few of those who came to know him afterwards ever heard how much grander had been his hopes, or how callously they'd been dashed.

In his emotional life, Sol was hardly luckier. As children, my brothers and I knew him as our bachelor uncle, a magical figure in our household; whenever he came by, he would bring with him an astonishing grab bag of windup toys and gadgets and then would spend hour upon hour with us telling stories, performing magic tricks, and listening to our views of the world, as sympathetic an adult as any we knew. When he finally did marry, at fifty-eight, it was for love, but one morning, three years into his new life, his wife did not wake up; it turned out that she had suffered an aneurysm. For the next nineteen months, while she lay in a coma, Sol all but lived at the hospital, hovering over her.

When at last she died, he returned home and resumed his existence much as before. However, by that time, his nieces and nephews were pretty well grown and living lives of our own, and few of us kept in touch with him.

At his funeral service, it was noted that several of my cousins had, as children, dubbed Sol "Uncle Pockets." I smiled, but the term triggered in me a powerful sense of regret. For, of course, I had been one of those who had never repaid him, even in small measure, for his generosity of spirit. In retrospect, it wasn't that I'd been especially callous; I simply hadn't thought.

Only once, toward the end, had I tried to make amends. Last December at a holiday family gathering, having recently read a friend's moving account of his trip to the ball park in the company of his elderly grandfather, I proposed a similar excursion to Sol. But when I called him last spring to make final arrangements, a few weeks before the start of the baseball strike, a month before his death, we ran into scheduling problems.

"You really wanna take me to a game?" he asked, seemingly incredulous.

"Yeah, I want to take you to a game."

He paused. "So when do you wanna do this?"

"I don't know, when's convenient?"

"Well, we can't do it this week. . . ."

"Why not?" I asked.

"The *Yankees* are in town. What'd ya think, I'm a front-runner?"

"Okay," I said, "how about next week? The Mets will be back next week."

"Next week I can't. I'm going to San Francisco next week."

I stopped. I was dimly aware that a cousin of mine was to be married in San Francisco the following week, but as far as I knew, no one in the New York branch of the family had even considered attending.

"*You're* going to San Francisco?" I asked now. "What does your doctor say?"

He came back at me fast, the message loud and clear. "I've never been to San Francisco," he snapped. "Someone's got to represent the family."

Living with Lies

This was going to be about something else. Indeed, I was halfway through a first draft of that other essay when, early on a muggy August evening, I stood on a New York subway platform flipping through a local daily and came upon a feature entitled THE TRAUMA OF WRITING "STILL MISSING." The article was about a person named Beth Gutcheon, a large photograph of whom appeared beneath the headline, and what I read so turned my stomach that I instantly lost interest in finishing the original piece.

To be sure, my stomach had been fully prepared to turn the moment I'd caught sight of the headline. *Still Missing* was, by then, a very familiar title. Like much of the reading public, I'd first become aware of Beth Gutcheon's book via a newspaper ad. The *Still Missing* ad, if you somehow missed it, pictured a child's sneaker, carelessly discarded, and was accompanied by the following copy: "Alex Selky, six years old, kissed his mother goodbye one morning and left for school . . . He did not come home."

Now, one does not have to be blessed with extraordinary insight to catch on to what was up here. A little over two years earlier, a very real little boy, named not Alex Selky but Etan Patz, had indeed kissed his mother goodbye, walked into the streets of lower Manhattan toward school, and disappeared. The story attracted enormous publicity, much of it focused on the heart-wrenching spectacle of Etan's parents pleading for their son's return, and for many months thereafter, even those New Yorkers who wanted to put the disquieting case out of mind had trouble doing so, for the city was awash in posters bearing the child's face beneath the words . . . STILL MISSING.

All of which would make this Gutcheon person's book (which, not so incidentally, was quickly sold to the movies and is said altogether to have earned its author $750,000) a pretty shabby enterprise to begin with. But, believe me, friends, this newspaper article was truly the topper. It was mostly devoted to describing how Ms. Gutcheon had *suffered* while composing her opus, so caught up had she become in her story. "It was so upsetting," she says at one point, describing an initial attempt to write the book in the first person, "I mean literally I was waking up at night, that I had to start over again in the third person."

And what of Etan Patz? After working my way through two columns of print, I started to think he might not be mentioned at all, so I began to scan the page for his name. Ah, there it was. Two-thirds of the way through the piece, the interviewer notes that "though the external details of the novel are different from those of the real-life incident," some people *do* see a similarity to the Patz case. However: "Gutcheon and her publisher are reluctant to make the connection," except that Gutcheon concedes that "if Etan hadn't disappeared it's very unlikely that I would have thought of this plot."

Do tell. As it happened, we are told, our novelist had a tough time coming up with an ending. Might that have had something to do with the fact that the Patz case remains unresolved? Perish the thought. "I think the reason was," Gutcheon says, "that in the process of writing this I had crossed so far over into being the person to whom this had happened, that it was harder and harder to deal with it as far as a detective story is concerned."

A few hours later that same evening, I was ten minutes into a tirade about all of this, reading from the article for illustration, when a friend stopped me cold with a laugh.

"What's so damn funny?" I demanded.

"You. Listen to yourself. I swear, you're going to give yourself a heart attack."

"But I'm mad. And I'm right!"

She shrugged. "Of course you're right. But so what? What good does your anger do?" She paused. "Christ, look around you. Don't tell me something like this surprises you. . . ."

"That's not the point. This woman actually thinks she can get away with spouting this kind of claptrap."

She smiled. "She can, obviously. Anyway, who knows, maybe this Gutcheon actually believes all that stuff herself."

In retrospect, I would guess that she does. Though she is, I surmise, an intelligent woman, and not unpleasant (for I also caught her on the "Today" show and in *People),* and not without a certain talent for prose (for, yes, before setting this down I felt obliged to read the offending volume), she does appear to have persuaded herself fully that, in fact, her book has nothing to do with exploitation. There are always credible reasons for one's behavior if one needs badly enough to find them.

But, frankly, all in all, I am a good deal less troubled by Gutcheon and her ilk than by the equanimity with which their self-serving nonsense tends to be swallowed by the rest of us. For, of course, frequently even the most obvious palaver passes us by unchallenged—accepted, if not at face value, at least without qualm. We have, in large measure, been morally neutralized, robbed of the capacity for appropriate reaction.

That, of course, has a lot to do with the sheer volume of stupidity, both malignant and benign, with which we are faced daily. We are so steeped in bull, so accustomed to babble pretending to meaning, that we have come to look upon fraudulence as a given of this society, like idiot situation comedies or tomatoes without taste. Not long ago, en route to a ball game, a friend of mine was in the course of explaining that his wife had been extremely irritable lately, when his six-year-old son abruptly weighed in from the back seat. "Mommy should try Sanka brand." We laughed—such is the latter-day notion of precocity—but an hour later my friend was wondering aloud whether an important part of the little bugger's body was well on its way to being snatched.

The choice of illustration is not, by the way, inadvertent, for I think it is television advertising, as much as anything else, that has served to so impair our critical faculties. The steady diet of cheerful, tuneful malarkey that we are force-fed hour after hour, year after year, serves as a kind of emotional anesthesia, conditioning us—*compelling* us—to distrust what we see and hear. Just yesterday, I spotted a commercial for Crest that asserted that there exists a new Crest, 30 or 40 percent more effective than the previous incarnation; in fact, the old Crest is all but shrugged off in the ad as having been snake oil in a tube. Well, if we were to take stuff like this at face value, what would all of us who've been using the old Crest for all these years—having been suckered in by the "Look, Ma, no cavities" campaign and the solemn assurances of the American Dental Associates—do with *that?*

Indeed, our failure to react to so much of what goes on around us is our most potent self-defense. A couple of years ago I sat in a restaurant with a psychologist friend of mine, watching an infant, slung over his mother's shoulder, crying uncontrollably. "Look at that," I remarked, "someday that guy could be auditing your tax return."

"Don't make fun of him," she said. *"That* is the absolutely honest reaction to much of what all of us go through every day. If the rest of us were as honest with our feelings, this restaurant would probably sound like a hospital nursery."

I expect that no one, with the possible exception of certain producers of bizarre documentary films, would wish quite that level of emotional candor upon the American public. But, at the same time, the capacity for indignation, even outrage, is to be cherished. I vividly recall how, in sixth grade, my classmates and I were incredulous when told of Hitler's use of the so-called Big Lie; how, we demanded, could reasonably intelligent people accept such palpable foolishness without question? Now I know. They didn't so much accept it as simply let it wash over them, like so many ads for a bad local brew.

Citing such an example in such a context is, I know, out of scale—like calling out a pack of attack dogs to deal with a peeping tom. In the world as we find it, we must, naturally, pick our battles. It is only the very rare TV ad, for example, that merits even a quarter ounce of bile. But, by the same token, it is terribly wrong to accept the genuine indecencies, large or small, as routine.

As for my dinner companion's nettlesome query—"What good does your anger do?"—well, in a pragmatic sense, I suppose not terribly much. There is precious little we can do, as individuals, to impede the general retreat from civility and compassion and taste. Never mind the Big Lies, even the *Still Missings*; the *New York Posts*, the formula films featuring one gruesome death per five thousand feet of celluloid will be with us a long, long time.

Finally, though, each of us bears the burden of his own integrity, and that means not only establishing for ourselves standards of behavior and abiding by them ourselves but fiercely defending them in the world at large. And it means, too, if it means anything at all, refusing to buy the after-the-fact disclaimers that every scoundrel in this society seems to carry as regulation gear.

It is, perhaps, only because even that minimal degree of discrimination is at odds with the norm that a vintage Mort Sahl routine, about Wernher von Braun, that good German gone straight, continues to play so wickedly well. "You know," Sahl would say, "they just made Von Braun's life into a movie. It's called *I Aim at the Stars*." A beat. "If you ask me, the title shoulda been *I Aim at the Stars—But Sometimes Hit London*."

We're
Number One

One evening last year, motel bound, I flicked on the Zenith and settled back for a spell of "Family Feud." Now, "Family Feud" may not pass for high art, not even in Burbank, but it makes for absolutely terrific sociology.

Midway through the show in question, for example, host Richard Dawson eyed a pair of members of that night's competing families and posed the following query: Based on one hundred people surveyed, "name something tourists go to see when they go to Paris." Lightning fast, hands reached for buzzers. "The Eiffel Tower!" came the first response and, indeed, it proved to have been the number one answer proferred by the anonymous sample. But—I'll assume here you know how this wonderful game is played— rather than try to come up with the remaining answers hidden on the big board, the lucky contestant, urged on by her brood, chose to pass the question on to representatives of the rival family. The first of these was obviously at a loss. "Uh . . . restaurants?" she offered finally. No luck. A huge X appeared on the screen, accompanied by a discordant NAAAAAH sound. It was now the turn of her sister, who agonized a long moment, made a tortured face, and was unable to make any response at all. NAAAAAH! Strike two. Sister number three was next, smugly waiting with what she thought was a surefire answer. "Clothes stores." NAAAAAH!

Now the hot potato went back to family number one, huddled in conference; if they could just come up with one of the mysterious sights of Paris, they would take a commanding lead in the game. At last, pressed by Dawson, they offered their tentative response. "The Lavooor Museum?"

Yes, indeed, there it was on the big board—"MUSE-UMS"—right after "FOLIES BERGERE" and "ARC DE TRIOMPHE."

Sitting in my motel room, disbelieving, I reached for a notepad. The Lavooor Museum? This I wanted verbatim. We were, after all, dealing with *Paris* here. For three hundred years the intellectual and cultural hub of the Western world. The Rights of Man. Molière. Voltaire. Napoléon. Hugo. The Dreyfus Affair. Paris is, arguably, the single most significant 41 square miles in the history of the planet. The Lavooor Museum?

But I should not have been surprised. With the possible exception of the French themselves, there exists no people in the industrialized world so utterly unconcerned with the world beyond its borders as we—nor one so contented in its ignorance. The message reaches us in earliest childhood and accompanies most of us to the grave: We Americans *matter* more than others; the way we do things is, by definition, the best way. Why, then, investigate other cultures? Why—as virtually any high school student will assert—even bother with another language? *Why?*

Of course, the case is occasionally made that at least we are less ethnocentric than we used to be. And it is true that just a generation ago, my elementary school friends and I used to congratulate ourselves over America never having lost a war, taking the liberty of discounting the War of 1812 as a "draw"; then came Vietnam. And many of us came to adulthood secure in the belief that American know-how was unmatched, and unmatchable, anywhere on the planet; now we own Sonys and Toyotas.

But that is an intellectual concession, this grudging recognition that maybe we are not without fault, after all. In our guts, we Americans know, *know,* that we have it all over other people.

God knows we continue to act that way. A foreign-born columnist for a New York weekly used to reprint tiny items from *The New York Times*—fillers, actually—reporting gargantuan disasters in faraway lands: a volcanic eruption that had killed a hundred thousand in Fiji, for instance, or a quake that had decimated an entire Indonesian province. His point, of course, was that all those lives mean a good deal less to us over here than yesterday's Mets game. Then there are the numberless American tourists who simply assume that the average foreigner in the streets speaks English—and that if he doesn't, talking a little louder will cause him to. Indeed, we even tend to have difficulty interesting ourselves in fictional beings who do not resemble ourselves. Martin Cruz Smith, the author of *Gorky Park,* reports that when he decided that his hero would be a Russian—this was, after all, a Russian tale—even people in the industry were incredulous. "We've set books every place in the world," says Smith with bemusement, "—in Borneo, in the Philippines, in South America, wherever—and the hero was always American, as if this were a natural state of affairs."

And why not? The assumption of our own superiority is implicit in virtually everything we read, or see, or hear, in the comic strips, in our political discourse, in the news media. Listen, for example, to CBS's Ed Bradley in a telecast entitled "The Saudis," in conversation with a prominent Saudi woman educator named Cecile Rouchdy.

Bradley: The work customs in your country. Women and men, even women doing secretarial work, can't work in the same office with a man.

Rouchdy: Because we are a segregated society.

Bradley: But you can?

Rouchdy: I am. I'm part of the segregation.

Bradley: And you think that's okay?

Rouchdy: Why not? Why should you always look upon it, whatever is different from your society as wrong?

Bradley: Well, look at Saudi Airlines, for example. There you have Saudi men working in the cabins as stewards. Saudi women are not permitted to do that.

Rouchdy: Yes.

Bradly: That doesn't make them equal.

Rouchdy: Why should—I mean, you keep talking about equality . . .

A moment later, seemingly oblivious to what he has heard, Bradley looks into the camera and intones, "It would be easy, by our standards, to judge Madame Rouchdy harshly, until you realize how far Saudi women have come in the last generation . . ."

Obviously, in the world as we find it, arrogance and parochialism can be a dangerous mix. There was a lot of snickering when an American President stunned a Mexican President with a remark about Montezuma's revenge, but the world view it represented was considerably less than amusing. Not, of course, that smug ignorance is the particular province of any party or administration. In testimony before the Senate Foreign Relations Committee, William P. Clark, Ronald Reagan's newly designated Deputy Secretary of State, conceded that he did not know the names of the prime ministers of South Africa or Zimbabwe, and in general demonstrated what *The New York Times* referred to as "an apparently thin grasp" of foreign policy. An Amsterdam daily called him a "nitwit," and *The Daily Express* of London ran a headline that read "Ask Me Another." Clark has since been promoted to National Security Advisor.

Over the years we have of course paid a devastating price—in Latin America, in the Near East, above all in Southeast Asia—for our ignorance of other cultures. Nor is there much evidence to suggest that we have absorbed the obvious lessons. Our tendency—often it has been more like a reflex—remains to support those culturally more like ourselves over those less like ourselves. We are now told, to evident general relief, that the "era of self-flagellation" is past—and within days we proceed to vote in the U.N., in callous disregard of African and Asian lives and against the whole rest of the world, in support of the aggressive marketing of infant formula.

But if there are likely to be continuing repercussions of a foreign policy based on such intractable ethnocentrism, so too do all of us whose understanding of other cultures is constrained by ignorance—whose curiosity is satisfied by the travel section of the Sunday paper, or the occasional outing at a foreign restaurant, or even what is picked up on quick hops abroad—suffer a loss in our own lives.

There is, for starters, no surer way of achieving perspective on one's own situation than by peeking at it, however briefly, through alien eyes. Not long ago, I met a visitor to these shores from Bangladesh, an earnest young man of boundless curiosity. During the course of a two-hour conversation, he asked many, many questions about the locals, expressing wonder whenever the talk turned to social values. "And old people?" he asked at one point. "In my country, all the generations live together—old, young, everyone in one house. I do not think it is that way here."

"Very rarely."

"Where do they live?"

"Sometimes alone, sometimes in special homes for old people." I noticed his consternation. "In Florida and Arizona, we have old-age communities that are really not so bad at all." I smiled. "They even have fun, I'm told. Golf. Shuffleboard. Dancing. Plenty of companionship. What could be better?"

He stared at me for a long moment. "That is one of the saddest things I ever heard, I think."

But more directly to the point, if the song lyric does not have it precisely right—if it is not so much "a big, wide, wonderful world" out there as much as a confusing and sometimes pitiless one—then our responsibility to face the world is all the greater. In shutting ourselves off, in living lives preoccupied with only the familiar and the routine, we become not only shallower but infinitely less vital—and usually less humane—human beings.

The evidence is too much with us. One September afternoon not long ago, for instance, I sat with a dozen relative strangers, watching, in an atmosphere of mounting excitement, as Nolan Ryan threw his record fifth no-hitter. Immediately following the game, still on NBC, on came the local news, and we all watched a report on those Vietnam veterans who continue to suffer the after-effects of exposure to Agent Orange. The effects are tragic in the extreme—there were shots of vets' children who'd been born with extreme deformities—and one could not but feel enormous sympathy for the angry ex-soldier, whose wife has had seven miscarriages, who said that he would *force* any son of his to go to Canada rather than allow him to fight in another such war. The reporter on the story, obviously moved, noted that there were as many as 210,000 Americans who'd served in 'Nam during the period the chemical was in use, and who might thus be concerned about its long-term consequences.

But not a word, not a syllable, was spoken in the entire segment, either by the reporter or any of the vets, on the effects the stuff is almost certainly having on the millions of Vietnamese who happened to live in Vietnam when we dropped it. Moreover, only one soul in my group even re-marked on the anomaly, and her complaint was met by palpable indifference on the part of the others.

But, as these things go, the point was brought home to

me with even greater force by a personal encounter. Laura, as we shall call her, is a young Argentinian, whom I came to know when she recently visited this country from her new home in Paris. She is immensely likeable, a person of humor, gentleness, reflection, and passion. But the story of her recent past, like those of so many of her countrymen, is a tale of such complexity and tragedy, it puts even the most baroque of our soap operas to shame. Laura's brother, an administrator at a mental hospital in Buenos Aires and the person she was closest to in the world, is dead, shot down on the street because of the progressive policies (i.e., the elimination of electroshock treatment and straitjackets) he was trying to institute in his domain. Her father, who witnessed the killing, had a heart attack and died half an hour later.

But there is much more. You see, Laura was in the United States to try and secure rights to see her son, now five years old, whom she has not laid eyes on in three years. The boy's father, Laura's ex-husband, is an American, who took the child from Argentina three years ago, shortly after Laura herself was arrested for her activities during her days as a medical student some years before; a militant, non-violent socialist, Laura had helped organize a dispensary in the slums of Buenos Aires. Such a past, in the Argentina of General Videla, was grounds for imprisonment, at the very least. Laura was, in fact, lucky; she spent only two months in one of those places euphemistically known as "detention centers," where torture is routine, and another year and a half in the relative comfort of a prison. On her release, she was permitted to leave the country for asylum in France.

Laura has discovered that her ex-husband has remarried and that the child has been told that the new wife is his natural mother. They have relocated, leaving word with his parents and friends that he intends for Laura to never see the child again.

That is a prospect which, at this writing, appears entirely likely, for Laura has found that it is not just one bitter former spouse, but an entire society that is arrayed against her. The courts have shown her precious little sympathy, for there, as almost everywhere else she turns in this country, she finds herself branded by her experiences. "The attitude is that I am something terrible—a terrorist, a murderer—or else why was I imprisoned," she says. "Not only do the authorities take this position, but so even do most people I meet socially. They might understand about Argentina in the abstract, particularly after Timmerman, but they simply cannot grasp it. The attitude here is that if a person is in jail, that person must be a criminal—and certainly an unfit mother."

All at once, Laura halts her narrative and tears of frustration well in her eyes. "Do you know that Timmerman offered to be tortured live over American television, just so Americans would understand what torture is?" She stops and shakes her head. "Who knows, maybe that is the only way Americans *can* understand, if they see it on TV."

Man
and Superman

"God, I feel like praying," moaned a friend of mine recently, in the midst of a particularly trying day. "What a miserable time not to believe in God!"

It is, of course, a thought that crosses the minds of many of us with some frequency. Instability and impermanence seem to be virtually the only constants in this land of ours, and the need of something larger than ourselves to hang on to, of something stronger and infinitely better, is literally primal. How could we not envy those granted the assurance of absolute faith? Nothing, absolutely nothing, could be more seductive.

Which is as concise an explanation as any for the phenomenon that Tom Wolfe has labelled the Third Great Awakening. The tidal wave pull of religion resurgent in this land has been such that many of the rest of us, on the outside looking in, often find ourselves assaulted by it.

Over the course of the months I wrote my *Esquire* column, there regularly arrived in my mailbox letters from believers, urging your correspondent to become same. Among the most disarming of these, and certainly among the gentlest in tone, was one from a lady in Ohio who acknowledged that, though not usually given to proselytizing, she had been quietly praying for me. "Please," she wrote, "do not dismiss this suggestion out of hand. Our adherence (or attempts, at least) to God's law have shown us many of the very things you write about to be true. Peace of mind is achieved by a simple, honest living and fair and loving dealings with the people we meet. You seem to recognize this, yet you're missing the joy of the Person who originated this orderly way of life, the Father, our God, and the revelation of His love, Jesus. . . ."

It is hard to be offended by a missive so illuminated by decency and altruism as that one. But the impulse behind it, its certainty about the correctness of its author's course and the implicit rejection of all others, remain unsettling.

For the believer, I know, certainty is the most bountiful of blessings, enabling him to see the world in terms of clear rights and obvious wrongs, rendering it an infinitely easier place in which to live. Upon getting religion, even so sleazy a soul as Chuck Colson, a man who should probably spend several lifetimes atoning for sins past, instantly assumed an air of moral rectitude.

But what, I think, too many of the faithful fail to recognize is that the longing for sounder values and simpler times is nearly pervasive. The rest of us feel the same damn way. Why shouldn't we? Enough years of fast food and raunchy skin books, enough years of amorality in high places and soaring crime, are enough to drive anyone to sober reflection.

The problem for those of us who do not believe, who cannot, constitutionally, bring ourselves to subscribe to the wholly unsubstantiated and seemingly bizarre theory of a pervasive spirit, but who, in fact, share the need to feel attached to a moral community, is that we have nowhere to go.

Once upon a time, of course, we did. Most of us now in our late twenties, or thirties, or forties can look back to a period when fulfillment was almost as easy to come by as it is for the most enthusiastic convert today, to a period when we, too, could measure ourselves by the quality of our belief. It is a supreme irony that the painful, chaotic Sixties—an era that is already being recalled as among the most traumatic in this country's history—was, for us, a time of immense purpose and fulfillment. I recall a friend of mine remarking, rather wistfully, in the midst of one of the endless antiwar strategy meetings at the small college we attended, that we would never feel as good about ourselves as we did then. At the time I didn't fully understand what he meant, but I do now; indeed, after all the hollow years since, after so many of us have moved from bitter disillusionment to gross self-indulgence, it is no wonder that salvation the old-fashioned way should look so appealing.

But it was no accident that we brought so much passion, so much raw emotion, to the civil rights and anti-Vietnam struggles. We were, many of us, raised very much in the humanist tradition, with a wide-eyed, nearly unshakable faith in the possibilities of humankind. From the sorry vantage point of here and now, that very phrase—"the possibilities of humankind"—sounds anachronistic, like something pulled from some nineteenth-century utopian tract. But the truth is, that belief was lodged in our hearts and guts, our own religion, our own means of reducing the world to primary colors. In the simplistic view of life we carried into adulthood, those representing religious orthodoxy tended, in fact, to be on the wrong side, arrayed against us as defenders (to borrow from the same utopian tract) of privilege and tradition. Those relatively few religious figures worthy of our esteem—the Berrigans, the militant nuns, the Martin Luther Kings—seemed religious in a most secondary way, for they made it equally clear that they believed in the power of human beings; indeed, they were more actively at odds with the religious traditionalists than anyone.

Lines of political demarcation have, of course, blurred considerably in recent years and, though many church hierarchies and the vast majority of Born Again types remain hostile to what are generally regarded as liberal values, more than a few others have embraced them. Within months of the formation of Moral Majority, Norman Lear created, in response, something called People for the American Way, numbering among its founders a variety of distinguished theologians, among them the president of the National Council of Churches, the executive director of the Lutheran Council, and Father Hesberg of Notre Dame. Moreover, a great many avowed humanists have, over the years, modified their harsh view of faith. "I don't like to admit it," says a friend of mine, a former SDS honcho, "but occasionally over the last few years, when things have gotten tough, I've found myself praying. It may or may not work but, hell, I'd rather be on the safe side."

Such an admission from such a source is rather refreshing, and probably bodes well for my friend's emotional survival. What is disheartening is that he, like so many of our generation, has along the way lost his other faith, the faith that once appeared likely to sustain him through a lifetime— the faith in his *own* possibilities. It is that sense of powerlessness, that absence of direction, that has so many of us running about pell-mell, searching for shelter.

A few weeks ago I received in the mail an intriguing press release, about a group of psychologists on the Upper West Side of Manhattan who practice what they call "Marxist" therapy. The reason for the press release was that some judge downtown, put off by the offending word, had ruled that these people were ineligible to treat a certain young man deemed by the court in need of therapy. But the details of the case were considerably less interesting than the description of the treatment itself. For the members of this group maintain that it is, above all, *society* that is desperately ill, that since we live in a world in which most people's values are hopelessly skewed it is emphatically *not* the therapist's function to help patients adjust to the prevailing norms; indeed, the therapist should, if he is genuinely interested in leaving patients feeling whole and at peace with themselves, encourage them to work, in any of a hundred ways, to alter society for the better.

That may sound naive, not to mention hopelessly out of sync with the times, but so too were those Americans who, a mere one hundred and fifty years ago, began devoting themselves to the abolition of slavery, or those who, within memory, had the gall to maintain, in the face of all evidence, that a climate might be created in which a Roman Catholic could be elected President. Nothing worthwhile has ever come easy, here or anywhere else. And frustration has never been a valid reason for abdicating personal responsibility.

To believe that there is a God in heaven is indeed a comforting thought, one that has sustained millions of souls in times even more desperate than these. There is much to be said for that. But, as a great many of the sincerely devout themselves recognize, as the Holy Books instruct, it is only a beginning.

There is a wonderful quotation attributed to the Spanish philosopher Unamuno, and, after much consideration, it was with this that I finally replied to the lady in Ohio, the one who had been making a point of praying for my soul. "To believe in God means to long for his existence and, more importantly, to *behave* as if He existed."